W9-BRT-955

JAPAN

Where East Meets West

by Judith Davidson

Dillon Press, Inc.   Minneapolis, Minnesota 55415

Photographs reproduced through the courtesy of the Consulates General of Japan in New York and Chicago. Cover photo by Carl Purcell.

Library of Congress Cataloging in Publication Data

Davidson, Judith.
    Japan, where East meets West.

    Bibliography: p. 139.
    Includes index.
    Summary: An introduction to the history and culture
of Japan including a discussion of Japanese in the
United States and appendices explaining hiragana symbols
and how to make a kimono.
    1. Japan—Juvenile literature.   [1. Japan] I. Title.
DS806.D36   952   82-7462
ISBN 0-87518-230-5   AACR2

Dillon Press, Inc., 500 South Third Street
Minneapolis, Minnesota 55415

Printed in the United States of America
        5 6 7 8 9 10 91 90 89 88 87 86

Contents

Fast Facts About Japan

Official Name: Japan; the Japanese also call their country Nippon or Nihon ("Source of the Sun").

Capital: Tokyo.

Location: North Pacific Ocean; the islands of Japan lie off the northeastern coast of Asia and face Russia, Korea, and China.

Area: 145,711 square miles (377,389 square kilometers); the four main islands—Hokkaido, Honshu, Shikoku, Kyushu—stretch about 1,300 miles (2,090 kilometers) from northeast to southwest. Japan has 5,857 miles (9,426 kilometers) of coastline.

Elevation: *Highest*—Mount Fuji, 12,388 feet (3,776 meters) above sea level. *Lowest*—sea level.

Population: *Estimated 1982 Population*—120,448,000; *Distribution*—76 percent of people live in or near cities; 24 percent live in rural areas; *Density*—826 persons per square mile (319 persons per square kilometer).

Form of Government: Constitutional monarchy; *Head of State*—emperor; *Head of Government*—prime minister.

Important Products: Rice, soybeans, tea; salmon, tuna; cameras, chemicals, electric and electronic devices, iron, motor vehicles, ships, steel, textiles.

Basic Unit of Money: Yen.

Major Languages: Japanese; English.

Major Religions: Shinto; Buddhism; Christianity.

Flag: Red sun against a white background.

National Anthem: "Kimigayo" ("The Reign of Our Emperor").

Major Holidays: New Year's Day—January 1; Emperor's Birthday—April 29; Constitution Day—May 3; Children's Day—May 5.

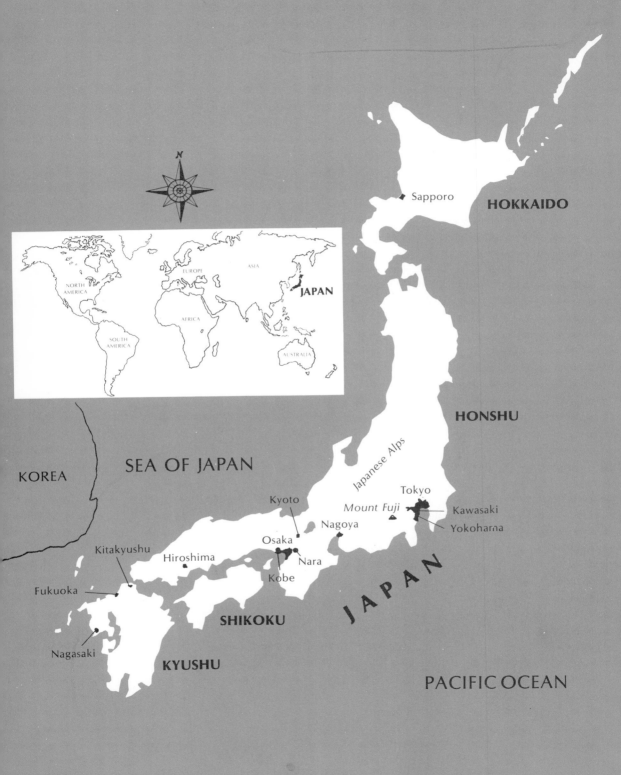

1. Japan: An Island Country

When travelers from the Western world first came to Japan, they were surprised by ways that were not at all like their own. The Japanese bowed to each other instead of shaking hands. Before entering a house, they took off their shoes. At mealtime they ate with chopsticks instead of forks. At night they slept on the floor instead of in beds. Even stranger to Western eyes, the Japanese read their books from the back to the front. And when they seemed to be waving "good-bye," they really meant "come here."

These ways are still a part of Japanese life, but so are baseball, television, computers, blue jeans, and rock music. A Japanese child may eat rice and bean soup with seaweed for breakfast, but then have chocolate milk and a hamburger for lunch.

Although the Japanese sometimes eat and dress like North Americans, they are an Asian people. Short and a little stocky, they have straight black hair. An extra fold of skin covers their eyelids.

The Japanese live in an island country, and most of them make their homes on four main islands. Hokkaido, the second largest, is in the north. Below it are Honshu, the largest island, and Shikoku, the smallest one. Farthest south is Kyushu, where bananas and oranges grow. Japan also has over 3,500 smaller islands. Yet the area of the whole country is only about the size of the state of California. No matter where you are in Japan, you are never more than one hundred miles from the ocean.

The sea has both brought people to Japan and kept them away from it. About 115 miles of water lie between Japan and its nearest neighbor, Korea. Early sailors traveling to or from the islands had to make a long and dangerous voyage. Many of them lost their ships or their lives to the sea.

The islands of Japan are part of a chain of volcanoes in the Pacific Ocean called the Ring of Fire. Long ago the earth beneath the ocean broke apart, and the pieces ground against one another. Soon hot liquid rock called lava poured out onto the ocean floor like molasses. When the lava rose above the water and cooled, wind and weather carved the hardened rock into jagged shapes. As a result, the Japanese islands are covered with sharp mountains, deep valleys, and gorges.

Of Japan's 265 volcanoes, about 50 are active. Thousands of hot springs also bubble up from the earth beneath the islands. Japanese families like to go to the hot springs for vacations.

Mount Fuji, or Fuji-san as the Japanese say, is

the most famous volcano in Japan. It has a smooth, beautifully shaped cone. Fuji-san hasn't erupted since 1707, though it sometimes gives off steam.

The Japanese worry about the danger of their islands breaking apart. Each day three or four earthquakes occur somewhere in Japan. Some Japanese think they can predict when the earthquakes will take place. They watch the goldfish in their ponds. When the goldfish start dancing and jumping strangely, these people believe an earthquake is coming.

Like the backbone of a dinosaur, the mountains of Japan run the whole length of the country. Called the "roof of Japan," they divide it into east and west.

The west side of the country faces Asia. Its coastline does not have many bays or inlets. In winter, winds from Siberia blow across the Sea of Japan, bringing rain and snow to the western side of the mountains. So much snow falls that it piles up to the overhanging roofs of the farmhouses. Summers on the west coast are warm but comfortable.

The eastern side of Japan, which faces the Pacific Ocean, has a great many bays and inlets. Winters here are mild because clouds from the west lose most of their rain and snow as they pass over the mountains. Summers, however, are hot and humid.

Children and adults look eagerly for the signs of each new season. They await the cherry blossoms of spring, the thunderstorms of summer, the full moons of fall, and the snowflakes of winter. But they feel sad as they watch each season passing.

Cherry blossoms come out in April. They are very beautiful, but they last only a short time. The Japanese believe that people's lives are like the cherry blossoms—beautiful but quickly gone.

When the cherry blossoms appear, everyone becomes excited. Reporters even talk about them on TV. Using maps, they cover the opening of the blossoms from south to north in such detail that their stories almost sound like war reports.

"The cherry blossoms opened in Okayama today," says the reporter. A close-up of blossoms unfolding on a tree appears on the TV. Then the camera moves back to the map.

"Blossoms will be opening tomorrow, experts predict. If it doesn't rain, then Gifu prefecture can expect them the day after tomorrow," he says, wrapping up the report.

During spring, many families go on *hanami*, flower-viewing trips. Maruyama Park in downtown Kyoto is a popular place to visit. People look at the flowers there and eat picnic lunches of rice balls. Unfortunately, the picnickers drop a large amount of garbage. At night park workers must clean up the mess before more flower lovers arrive.

Viewing the beautiful cherry blossoms is a popular springtime activity in Japan.

April also means the start of the new school year. The Japanese school year begins in the spring instead of the fall. On June 1, children whose schools require uniforms are allowed to start wearing their summer outfits at school. But just when the sunshine brings warmer days, in rolls the first thunderstorm of *tsuyu*, the rainy season.

Tsuyu, the Japanese believe, comes in and goes out with a big thunderstorm. The rains fall on every island except Hokkaido and last until early July. During the rainy season, the weather becomes hot and muggy. This weather helps the rice seedlings to begin growing in flooded fields called paddies.

When tsuyu leaves, the thunder growls across the paddies and rushes into the steep mountains. Pouring rain fills the narrow rivers. Mothers grab their children and run inside. Water slides off the city buildings in sheets. But the downpours soon end, and summer comes for good.

Summer is the time for bug hunting. Net in hand, children search the grasses by ponds and temples for beetles and butterflies.

August 15 is *Obon*, the festival of the dead. On the last day of the festival, bonfires are lighted to help the spirits of the dead find their homes. As with Labor Day in the United States and Canada, Obon means that summer is over.

Early autumn is a warm, slow time. In the gardens, the humming of large beetlelike bugs called cicadas sounds like a buzzing electric wire.

Dangerous storms called *typhoons* also come to Japan in the fall. Like hurricanes, they bring strong winds and rains, and sometimes even tidal waves. Three or four typhoons reach the southern island of Kyushu every year. At times they move north as far as the cities of Kyoto or Tokyo.

Fall is the time for *tsukimi*, moon watching. At the end of October the moon is full and white. The Japanese go to beautiful places—temples, river banks, or gardens—to watch it shine down. But when they look into the night sky, they don't imagine that they see the face of the man in the moon. Instead, they see a rabbit making rice cakes.

Fall is a good time to go to the mountains to pick mushrooms. The favorite mushroom, *matsutake*, is very big and grows only in pine forests. Matsutake is hard to find.

When winter comes, you often hear the words, *Nan mai o kitte iru* ("How many layers are you wearing")? That's how grandmothers greet each other on the street in winter. Most Japanese houses don't have furnaces, and it's hard to keep warm. Although some rooms have a small oil heater, the *kotatsu* keeps most Japanese warm.

A kotatsu is a low table. Underneath it is a special electric heating bulb protected by a grill. The bulb's heat is kept in by a quilt hanging over the table. People can sit with their legs under the quilt and stay warm and cozy.

On New Year's Eve the big temple bells ring out. Children, parents, and grandparents dress in their best *kimono*, a traditional Japanese robe. At midnight they walk to the shrine to pray for the new year.

The old year gives way to the new. The seasons pass. For hundreds of years the Japanese have taken joy in these changes.

The change of seasons is especially important to farmers because bad weather can damage their rice crops. If the rains are late, the rice will be slow to start growing. If a typhoon comes, the rice may be broken down and ruined. In either case, people will go hungry. For in Japan the word for rice, *gohan*, is also the word for meal. When there is no rice, there is no meal.

Although almost two-thirds of Japan is covered by mountains, any land that will grow food is farmed. Every available valley or plain is divided into rice fields. The steep sides of hills are also plowed, or terraced, to grow rice.

Still, the Japanese cannot produce all the food

they need. They have to buy much of it from other countries. Buying so much food worries them, and they are trying to grow more. But cities, factories, airports, and golf courses take land, too. Some farmers can get more money by selling their land than by growing crops on it.

Air pollution is another problem. In the large cities there are often air pollution warnings. Health authorities tell parents and schools not to let children play outside during these times.

Air pollution is a serious problem in Japan, especially in or near large industrial centers.

Air pollution is a serious problem in Japan because millions of people live so closely together. In fact, Japan is one of the most crowded countries in the world. Everyone in it would like more space. About the size of California, Japan has half as many people as the United States. Only a small number of these people live in the mountains. Most of them make their homes in coastal areas. In fact, over 20 million Japanese live in eight coastal cities: Fukuoka, Kawasaki, Kitakyushu, Kobe, Nagoya, Tokyo, and Yokohama.

Because the country is so crowded, Japanese houses are very small, and people usually don't have their own rooms. Many families have only one or two rooms to live in. Heavy quilts, called *futon*, are kept folded up in a closet during the day. At night everyone sleeps together on the floor in these quilts. Sleeping in this way is comfortable, though, because the floor is covered with straw mats known as *tatami*.

The walls inside the houses are sliding doors made of paper. You can hear most sounds through them. The walls between houses are thin, too. It's hard to keep secrets in Japan.

No matter where you live in Japan, you can hear the clacking sound of trains. Electric trains run from the suburbs to the city. Diesel trains travel through the countryside. Japan has one of the fastest trains in

As this scene at Shinjuku Station in Tokyo shows, Japan is one of the most crowded countries in the world.

the world. Called the *Shinkansen*, or "Bullet Train," it goes 130 miles an hour.

Japanese children like to watch the trains go by outside their homes. Inside they like to play with pets. Their houses, however, are too small for them to keep dogs and cats. Instead, the children make pets of turtles, crickets, large, horned cockroaches, and goldfish.

Unlike the small animals children keep as pets, wild animals are hard to find in Japan. Bears can sometimes be seen in Hokkaido, and deer, wild pigs, foxes, and badgers live deep in Japan's forests. A herd of tame deer wanders freely through the national park at Nara.

Japan has one animal that is not found anywhere else in the world. It is a special monkey that can survive in cold and snow. Called a snow monkey, it lives only in northern Honshu.

Tokyo, the busy capital city of Japan, is also found on Honshu. It is the home of Emperor Hirohito, Japan's most important leader. The Japanese love and respect their emperors. They even count their ages by the number of years an emperor rules. Hirohito has been emperor since 1926, and he is now in year fifty-seven of his rule, or *Shōwa*.

If you are eleven years old, and you were born in 1970, then you were born in Showa 45. If you had

Superexpress trains, such as this one which runs from Tokyo to Osaka, are a common sight in Japan.

been born in 1868, your birthday would have been in *Meiji* 1. Emperor Meiji, Hirohito's grandfather, began ruling Japan in 1868.

The Japanese emperor has no power to make decisions for the people and the government. This power belongs to the Japanese Diet, which is like the American Congress. People from each area of the country are elected to the Diet. These people meet in Tokyo to make laws and solve Japan's problems.

The Japanese lawmakers know what their own people want and need. But living in an island country has made most Japanese shy toward other peoples. They feel as you might have felt when you moved to a new neighborhood or started at a new school. When they see strangers, the Japanese wonder: Will these people like me? What will we have in common? Will they want to be friends? Will these strangers laugh at the way I do things, or will they want to understand?

Despite being shy, the Japanese are very proud of their land. They want to share their ways and learn about the ways of other countries, too.

2. *Learning To Be Japanese*

Tea. Think about the word. What thoughts pop into your mind? Tea bag is probably the first. You may also think of tea as that bitter drink that adults have for breakfast. If you lived in Japan, the word tea would bring many ideas to mind. Here are three scenes you might imagine.

Scene One: You are riding in a train, early in the morning. Passing by a steep hillside, you see an *ojii-san*, an old farmer. His back is half bent from long years of heavy work. Standing at the top of the hill, he is looking over his tea field. The tea grows in long rows up and down the hill. The small leaves on the neatly shaped hedges sparkle in the sun. The old man feels good as he admires the green tea, wet from watering. His family's fields have been famous for hundreds of years.

Scene Two: You are walking down a covered shopping street in the busy city of Osaka. The smell of roasting tea draws you toward one shop. All grades of tea are sold here. The best tea is a green powder as fine as gold dust. Lower grades are much less fine; some have barley mixed in with the tea.

Scene Three: Dinner is almost over. To help you

Summer is the time for picking tea leaves, here being done by women in Shizuoka Prefecture, one of Japan's tea centers.

finish off that last bowl of rice, your mother pours tea over what remains. This dish is called *O-chazuke*, green tea over rice. As far as you're concerned, this is the best part of the meal.

The aroma of tea is always in the air. The Japanese drink it every day. They also use tea in a very special ceremony. In this ceremony a person learns to behave well, to enjoy nature, and to share a quiet moment with friends. Nature, good behavior, and friendships—these three things are very important to all Japanese.

Let's take part in a tea ceremony. It is held in a tea house, a one-room building set in a special garden. First, take off your shoes, leaving them outside the tea house. Then step into the room with the other guests. Like you, everyone will be wearing a *kimono*. (If you are interested in buying or making your own kimono, see Appendix B, p.129.)

The Japanese often dress in a kimono for special occasions such as the tea ceremony. It is a simple robe with long square sleeves that is tied with a wide sash called an *obi*. The kimono is worn with *tabi*, ankle high white socks which are divided at the big toe of each foot. Guests at the tea ceremony also hold a small folding fan and carry *kaishi*, special paper napkins.

Once inside the tea house you kneel on the

tatami-covered floor. Now you must admire the *tok-onoma*, a small opening in the corner of the room. Inside it hangs a beautiful painting or a piece of writing done on rolled paper. There is a flower arrangement beneath the paper.

Looking at the tokonoma helps put you into the mood of the tea ceremony. If it's October, you might see chrysanthemums, the last flowers of the garden. The writing might be a poem by a famous poet.

Bowing to the tokonoma, you now take your place. As you watch, your host or hostess carefully prepares the tea. Nowadays many more young girls and women come to the tea ceremony than boys or men, although once it was an art that samurai warriors studied.

Your hostess wipes the tea bowl, which has no handles, with a special paper. Now she measures the powdery green tea into the bowl with a scoop. Then she pours in hot water with a ladle and mixes the tea with a fine bamboo brush. The tea foams like lightly beaten eggs.

Before you drink, you admire the tea bowl, turning it carefully in your hands. Smooth and round, the bowl is pleasant to touch. You think about the potter who shaped this unusual piece, and all the people who have touched it and drunk from it.

After you drink, you wipe the spot where your

Many young Japanese girls are trained in the ancient art of the tea ceremony. Here the hostess is wiping the tea bowl before mixing tea in it.

lips touched the bowl with your kaishi. Then you pass the tea to the next guest.

Tea is both a drink and a way of life. Even Japanese who don't study the tea ceremony are affected by it. For example, many Japanese table manners come from the tea ceremony.

Gift giving is also important in Japan. The Japanese believe that you should never visit someone empty-handed. For this reason even the smallest railroad station always has a cake shop where you can pick up a nice present. You must choose the right type of gift, though. If you give too much or too little, you and your host will be uncomfortable.

The Japanese also buy gifts whenever they take a trip. Even if they only travel to a temple in a nearby town, they pick up an *o-miyage*, or souvenir, for close friends or family.

Friends are important in Japan, but parents are even more important. *On* is the special Japanese word for the debt that children owe their parents for raising, feeding, and loving them. Every Japanese child knows the saying, "On is higher than the mountains and deeper than the seas." The oldest boy in a family grows up knowing that he will take care of his parents in their old age.

In Japan a person without a family has a difficult life. Japanese grandmothers sometimes refuse to go shopping alone. Someone from their family, either a daughter-in-law or a grandchild, must go with them.

"If I'm alone, people will think that I don't have any family. They will think that there is no one to care for me. That would embarrass me," a grandmother may say. Nothing worries the Japanese more than being shamed or losing respect. They don't want other people to laugh at them or treat them badly.

Losing respect has been the subject of many plays. And oh how the Japanese love plays! They have a special kind of puppet show called *Bunraku.* Puppets in this show are not moved by pulling wires. Instead, they are handled by people who can be seen by the audience. You might think that seeing the puppeteers would ruin the play. However, these performers work so carefully and skillfully that the audience forgets about them and watches the play.

In Bunraku plays the actors are wooden puppets. Two other types of plays, *Noh* and *Kabuki*, are performed by human actors. Yet all three kinds of plays share many of the same stories. These stories deal with war, love, families, famous people in Japanese history, and, of course, losing respect. Many of the stories end sadly, and their heroes are often losers rather than winners. The Japanese like stories that leave them crying.

The Forty-seven Rōnin is a very famous play. It

has been made into a movie several times. In the story, forty-seven samurai warriors plot to kill a ruler who has caused their lord's death. Their plot succeeds, but they are forced to take their own lives because they have broken the law. They accept this punishment because it was their duty to protect their lord. If they hadn't killed the ruler, they would have lost respect, something far worse to them than death.

Plays, poems, stories, and movies are possible because of writing. Until A.D. 500 the Japanese didn't have a written language. About that time, many Koreans and some Chinese crossed the sea to Japan. These people brought the Chinese writing system with them.

Because the Japanese saw how important writing could be, many of their leaders learned Chinese. Then they could send messages and information to anyone else who could understand the Chinese characters.

Unfortunately, Japanese and Chinese are very different languages. Since people didn't want to speak Japanese and write Chinese, they needed a system to write the Japanese sounds. After a time they developed a kind of writing called *hiragana*. It was based on a set of simple Chinese characters which stood for the Japanese sounds.

Women in ancient Japan wrote in hiragana because they were not taught Chinese characters.

Famous actor Mitsugoro Bando plays the role of Ikyu, an aged warrior in the play Sukeroku, *one of Japan's most popular kabuki plays.*

Some of the most famous books and poems of ancient Japan were written by women—Sei Shonagon, Lady Murasaki Shikibu, and Ono-no-Komachi.

Today the Japanese way of writing is a mixture of Chinese characters and Japanese hiragana. It's not easy to learn. Japanese children must spend many more hours learning their writing system than you do learning to spell. (See Appendix C, p. 130 for a list of the hiragana symbols.)

Katakana is another way to write the Japanese sounds. You can think of katakana as being like printing and hiragana as being like handwriting. Katakana is hard and square; hiragana is smooth and flowing. However, katakana is used only for foreign words and in telegrams.

Speaking Japanese is easier than writing it. However, you must choose your words carefully. For instance, when you speak to your father you call him *otōsan*. When you speak to your friends about your father, you refer to him as *chichi*. Otosan is a word of respect and praise, and you don't want to embarrass your friends by praising your father too much. They would think you have no sense of politeness.

Being polite is important because in a crowded country like Japan people must try to get along with each other. Japanese children have to learn to control their feelings. They have no rooms to run to if they become angry. And the walls in their houses are so thin that everyone can hear them if they quarrel or cry.

To get along in Japan, people cannot insist on having their own way. In a Japanese family, the parents' opinion always carries the most weight. In other groups like clubs and offices, however, everyone must agree to accept the same ideas or to do the same things.

Suppose that people want to choose a name for a town baseball team. In the United States, several names might be suggested and then voted on. The name that received the most votes would be used, because in America the majority rules. But in Japan the discussion would last until everyone appeared to have accepted one name. The Japanese don't want anyone to be left out or to have hurt feelings.

The Japanese believe that it is better to agree than to quarrel. Their way of thinking is interesting to think about. Perhaps you can learn from them by comparing other Japanese ways to your own. Then the next time you think of tea you won't stop at tea bag. You'll also think of a tea ceremony in a quiet garden.

3. The Japanese Past

Where do I come from? Where did my father and mother come from? You have probably asked yourselves these questions. The Japanese, too, look to the past to understand who they are, and why they do things the way they do.

People first came to Japan from Asia during the great Ice Age. They were able to cross a natural land bridge formed when the ice had lowered the sea level. The Ice Age is the only time that Japan has not been an island country.

Because they live on islands, the Japanese have not had much contact with other peoples. Only for short periods of time have they been able to meet new peoples and take in new ideas. Yet even then they have always changed what they learned and borrowed from other countries into something very Japanese.

The earliest settlers in Japan were probably the *Ainu*. These people may have crossed to Japan when there was still a land bridge from Asia. No one can say for sure when they arrived in Japan or where they came from, however.

The next settlers, the *Yayoi*, came by boat.

These two Ainu men are boating on Lake Akan in northern Hokkaido. The Ainu, a separate people from the Japanese, were probably the first settlers in Japan.

During the Yayoi age, visitors from Korea and
China brought new ways and ideas to Japan. The
people of the Yamato nation, as Japan was then
called, borrowed a writing system, crafts, and Buddhism, a religion from India, from these visitors.

As time passed, some Yayoi families became
more powerful than others. The strongest chiefs built
large graves, or tombs, for themselves. Around these
tombs they put red, baked clay statues called *haniwa.*
Many of the haniwa look like armored soldiers who
are sitting on horses. Bronze mirrors and swords were
also put in the tombs.

Early Japanese society was divided into families
called clans. According to an ancient legend, one of
these clan chiefs, Jimmu Tenno, became the first
emperor. In early Japan, women could rule as
empresses, too.

Around A.D. 600 a prince named Shōtoku came to
power. Shotoku was not the emperor. All his life he
ruled through Empress Suiko. In fact, for most of
Japanese history the country's real ruler has not been
on the throne. Instead, power has been held by the
strongest clan chief, a warlord, or, in recent years, the
Diet.

Prince Shotoku accepted the ideas of Gautama
Buddha, a philosopher and holy man from India. He
built temples where people could worship Buddha.

Prince Shotoku (center) brought Buddhism and Chinese ways to Japan. He is pictured here with his son (left), and his brother (right).

At this time, though, the Japanese did not believe in only one god. According to Shinto, their own religion, there were many gods, some good and some evil. Shinto legends also said that the emperor's family was descended from the sun goddess, Amaterasu, and many ruling Japanese families believed that they had Shinto gods for ancestors.

Shotoku did not try to destroy the Shinto religion. Yet his strong support for Buddhism made it a part of Japanese life. Today many Japanese combine Shinto and Buddhist beliefs, worshiping the Shinto gods at shrines and Buddha at temples.

The prince also read all he could about the Chinese government and its laws. He sent several groups to China to learn how the Chinese lived. These groups brought back books, art, music, dances, and many other things.

Prince Shotoku ruled for nearly thirty years. Later, the Fujiwara family held the throne for about four hundred years during a time called the Heian period. Like the time of King Arthur's court at Camelot, the Heian period was a special age. For the first time, the Japanese wrote about themselves in novels, diaries, and essays. This writing was only done by rich and powerful people, though. Since poor people were not taught to write, little is known about their lives.

When the Fujiwara family gained power, Japan's

This great statue of Gautama Buddha, the Indian philosopher and holy man, was built in Kamakura, Japan, around the middle of the thirteenth century. It is thirty-seven feet high (not counting the base) and weighs 124 tons.

capital was moved from Nara to Kyoto, a city in a wooded valley on the Kamo River. Kyoto was designed like the Chinese capital of Ch'ang-an. The main streets were laid out like a huge checkerboard. Many of Kyoto's streets still have the same names that they did a thousand years ago.

People believed in magic during the Heian period. The movement of the stars guided their lives. They believed that marrying on certain days or traveling in certain directions would bring them good luck. They also thought that studying numbers could tell them what the future might bring.

Wearing correct clothing was very important to the people of this time, too. Wealthy women wore a *junihitoe*, a dress made of twelve kimonos carefully layered over one another. The rules about choosing and combining colors for the dress were very strict. Each shade of color had to peek out correctly from the sleeves.

While the court in Kyoto enjoyed life in beautiful palaces, other Japanese were not so lucky. Outside of the capital many changes were taking place. Life was wild and dangerous far from the main cities because bandits attacked travelers along roads and in the forests.

When the streets of Kyoto finally became unsafe, Japan's rulers hired warriors to protect them and their palaces. Even the temples had armies of warrior monks. These soldier priests often battled with other temples.

Two families, the Tairas and the Minamotos, made a business of protecting the royalty. After a time these two families grew stronger than the rulers. Then the real contest for power was between them.

The two families fought a terrible war in the twelfth century. In the end, Minamoto-no-Yoritomo, the winner, set up a new capital in Kamakura, near today's Tokyo. Like other Japanese rulers, he kept the emperor in Kyoto and told him what to do. Yoritomo was called the *shōgun*. (In Japan the family name comes before the given name. We would write Yoritomo Minamoto instead of Minamoto-no-Yoritomo.)

Yoritomo might not have won without the help of Yoshitsune, his younger brother. Songs, novels, plays, and puppet shows have been written about Yoshitsune. He is a very important hero to the Japanese.

Yoshitsune's story began when Taira-no-Kiyomori defeated Yoshitsune's father in battle. All of the Minamoto family were killed, except for the youngest sons and their mother. Yoshitsune was sent to a temple north of Kyoto to become a priest. Legends say that at night he would sneak away to the

Yoritomo Minamoto, brother of the legendary Yoshitsune Minamoto, became Japan's first shogun in A.D. *1192.*

mountains. There the *tengu*, magical creatures with long noses, taught him how to become a warrior and to use a sword.

As a teenager, Yoshitsune escaped to the north of Honshu, the main Japanese island. When his brother Yoritomo attacked the Tairas, Yoshitsune joined the fight.

Yoshitsune was an excellent general, both daring and smart. Again and again he planned battles that surprised the enemy. At Ichinotani, near the present-day city of Kobe, the Tairas thought they had found a safe place to hide. In front of them was the ocean; behind them were steep mountains. And yet clever Yoshitsune found a way to attack them. He led a band of men on horseback down cliffs so steep that monkeys would even think twice about climbing down them. The Tairas were caught completely by surprise, and Yoshitsune won a great victory.

When the Minamotos finally defeated the Tairas, the jealous Yoritomo turned on his brother. He made Yoshitsune an outlaw and chased him and his men to the north. In their last battle, Yoshitsune and his family took their own lives, and his warriors died protecting the family.

The Japan that Yoritomo and his sons ruled was not the Japan of today. Hokkaido was still outside of the country. The rest of the nation was divided into states ruled by separate kings, called *daimyo*. The daimyo were loosely organized under Yoritomo, the shogun. The daimyo placed soldiers at barriers on the main roads into their lands and used check points to guard against surprise attacks.

Each daimyo had soldiers known as *samurai*. Japanese children know as much about the samurai as American children know about cowboys. Cowboys lived by the "Code of the West"; the samurai by *bushido*, the "Way of the Warrior." Both cowboys and samurai were supposed to be brave, true to their friends, and unafraid of death.

The Japanese compare the samurai's life to cherry blossoms. Both are beautiful and pure, and both can quickly pass away. Many samurai studied *Zen*, a form of Buddhism. Zen helped the warrior fight his enemies and face death.

With the help of the samurai, the warlords stopped other Asian peoples from coming to Japan. But as time passed, the warlords began to fight among themselves, and foreigners gained entry into the country. In 1543 Portugese traders became the first Europeans to land in Japan. Soon after them came Catholic priests. The Japanese called the Europeans *Nambanjin*, which means "Southern Barbarians."

The priests sent letters back to Europe about Japan. These letters were printed and read by many people. Jesuit priests opened a press in Japan and printed the first Japanese dictionaries. Europeans also brought the first guns to the islands.

Very few people know that the priests brought a group of Japanese to Europe in 1582. Four young Christian men from Kyushu, sons of wealthy daimyo, were taken to Spain and Italy. People in Europe had their first chance to meet the Japanese, and the young men became the first Japanese to see Europe. They even visited the pope in Rome.

Europeans were not the only people the Japanese learned about. Japanese pirates and traders also brought back news of other lands when they sailed the South Pacific seas.

Japan was now ruled by Tokugawa Ieyasu, a cruel man who had fought to become the chief daimyo. In Ieyasu's view, any new ideas were dangerous. He didn't want the priests to teach Christianity or the Japanese to travel to Europe. Ieyasu was also afraid that the Europeans might try to attack Japan. He thought the Catholic priests were spies for the European kings. In 1614 he closed Japan to Europeans, allowing only the Dutch to have a trading station on a small island in Nagasaki harbor. Death was now the punishment for being a Christian. Death was also the punishment for leaving Japan and trying to return.

Ieyasu divided the Japanese into four groups:

priests, warriors, farmers, and merchants. He gave each group strict rules to follow and said that only people from the same group could marry each other.

The nearly three hundred years of the Tokugawa period were in many ways like the Dark and Middle Ages in Europe. During these times, a few people owned most of the land, and they used it to force other people to serve them. However, Japanese farmers were better off than European serfs, who were treated like slaves. They were also better educated and had more rights than the serfs. Their villages had strong forms of self-government.

The common people in the Tokugawa period are written about in novels and diaries, and they are shown in pictures. Their appearance in books and paintings tells us that Japan was slowly changing.

One reason for this change is that merchants were becoming more important than warriors. Soy sauce sellers, rice wine merchants, kimono makers, and timber dealers were growing very powerful, and the samurai were often in debt to them. Only the samurai clans that learned to be good at business survived after the Tokugawa period.

The Tokugawa family was forced to give up its control of Japan by the Satsuma and Chosu clans. In 1867 they overthrew Tokugawa Yoshinobu, the fifteenth shogun, and asked Emperor Mutsuhito to rule

Japan. Mutsuhito agreed, and the change in power, called the Imperial Restoration, was announced on December 9, 1867. Known as Emperor Meiji (*Meiji* means "Enlightened Rule"), Mutsuhito became one of Japan's greatest rulers. He used his power to help make Japan into a modern nation.

Under Emperor Meiji, Japan opened its doors to the world once again. New ideas and ways from Europe and America were borrowed, argued about, and tested. The Japanese liked some new things and disliked others. But in the end they adopted many new ways from the Western world in order to become a modern country.

Between 1867 and World War II, Japan became one of the world's leading powers. It changed itself from a land of farms into a nation of factories. Yet many Japanese, including the country's military leaders, did not like this change. They thought Japan was becoming too much like Western nations. They also thought Japan could not protect itself from attack, keep its factories going, or find places to sell its products unless the army took control of the country.

During the 1930s, these military leaders sent Japan's armies to take land in Manchuria and other parts of northern China. They said they were creating a safety zone around Japan, but they also wanted oil, rubber, and minerals for their country's factories.

Emperor Hirohito and other government leaders may not have approved the actions taken by the army. But the victories it won in China led most Japanese to support the military men, who soon took control of Japan. They signed treaties to support Germany and Italy in time of war and sent Japanese soldiers to seize land in what is now Vietnam, Cambodia, and Laos.

The United States challenged these actions by stopping shipments of oil, scrap iron, and steel to Japan. Because the army leaders thought that Japan could not do without these materials, they decided to go to war. On December 7, 1941, Japanese planes made a surprise attack on the American naval base at Pearl Harbor in Hawaii. Following it, the two countries fought for four long years.

Then on August 6, 1945, the United States dropped an atom bomb on Hiroshima, a city in southern Honshu. Soon afterwards, it dropped another atomic bomb on Nagasaki, a city on the west coast of Kyushu. These bombs forced Japan to give up. Too many of its people had been killed, and too many others were facing starvation.

The United States Army stayed in Japan from the war's end in 1945 until 1952. General Douglas MacArthur and other Americans helped to rebuild the country.

Even today some Japanese are dying slow, painful deaths from atomic radiation because they lived in or near Hiroshima or Nagasaki. In Hiroshima a park has been built where the bomb fell. A special place in it honors the children who were killed. The Japanese make paper cranes, called *tsuru*, which they hang in this place. The cranes are gifts for the lives and spirits of the children.

Modern Japan is a busy country. Since World War II it has rebuilt its major cities, adopted a democratic form of government, and become the leading industrial nation in Asia. In fact, Japan's factories produce more goods than every country except the United States and the Soviet Union. The ships, cars, chemicals, tools, cameras, electronic devices, and other products that Japan sells abroad have made it very wealthy.

Thirty years ago Japan received help from the United States to rebuild its country. Today it is able to give help—billions of dollars each year—to many poorer nations. Giving this aid is a sign that Japan is taking on a new role of leadership in the world community.

The Japanese still have an emperor, Hirohito, but he has no power. In fact, Hirohito is best known as a marine biologist, a scientist who studies the sea. The real power is held by elected officials who deal with

Japan's problems and make laws to protect the people's rights.

These officials realize how much their country depends on the rest of the world. It must buy oil for its cars and factories, and timber for its buildings. It must also buy fruits, vegetables, rice, and meat to feed its people. To pay for these things, Japan must sell its products to other nations and make treaties with them about fishing, trading, and land rights.

Japan will never again be able to close its doors to the world as it did under Tokugawa Ieyasu. It needs to trade with other nations as well as learn from them. Yet the Japanese will not forget their own country's past. They have long been a separate people living in an island country, and they will try to keep their special ways.

4. A Land of Many Legends

Japan is a land of many legends. Every village is alive with stories. An unusual rock, a large old tree, a famous person who passed by the way, or village gossip—all of these can be made into legends.

One reason Japan has so many legends is that it is an island country. Japan has been a stable place to live, and there have been few outsiders. Each village has had time to develop its own stories.

Local legends have a special meaning to the people who live in a village. They tie the people to the place. Legends are one reason that the Japanese people have such strong feelings about their hometowns.

Some local legends deal with animals that villagers often see—deer, badgers, mice, and birds. None of these animals appears in more stories than the fox, though.

Kitsune, the fox, is quite a mischief maker. People blame many things on this sly creature. When someone goes mad, the Japanese sometimes say that a fox has taken over the person's mind. They also say that a fox will trick people by pretending to be human. However, foxes will also repay humans with great kindness when they are grateful for a good deed.

Many stories tell about a drunken villager coming home alone late at night who is stopped by a stranger. The stranger leads him off his path to a place where a lively party is going on. The villager eats, drinks, and makes merry. When he wakes up in the morning, he finds that he is lying alone in the middle of the field. The stranger of the night before had really been kitsune, and the evening was a dream created by the mischievous animal.

The fox is also believed to be a messenger of Inari, the rice god. Long ago villagers often saw foxes in the fall when they harvested the rice. They came to believe that Inari had sent kitsune to check on their harvest and report back to him. Today you will see many statues of foxes at the shrines where Inari is worshiped.

Many words and sayings have come from the legends about foxes. For example, a Japanese might use the words *kitsune ga bakasaseta* ("to be tricked by a fox"). This phrase means, "I've been fooled."

Kitsunebi, fox light, is the Japanese word for a will-o-the-wisp, a strange darting light that sometimes appears in the woods at night. People in Japan think that the fox uses this light to lead a traveler off a path.

The Japanese have also named one of their dishes after the fox. This dish is made of large white noodles topped with *aburage*, fried soybean cake. It is called *kitsune udon*, fox noodles, because people believe that aburage is one of the fox's favorite treats.

The fox is not the only famous animal in Japan. The Japanese have also named each year after an animal—Rat, Ox, Tiger, Rabbit, Dragon, Snake, Horse, Sheep, Monkey, Rooster, Dog, and Boar. In Japan you are born in the year of the Rabbit, Horse, or Rooster rather than under the sign of Taurus, Virgo, or Gemini.

In addition to telling stories about animals, villagers have made up tales about imaginary creatures. Some of these tales deal with devils that have three fingers, three toes, and, sometimes, three eyes and horns. Called *oni*, these creatures can also fly if they need to make a fast getaway.

Yamauba are very scary. They are lady goblins who hide deep in the mountains. Some yamauba are old and have stringy white hair; others are like pretty snow witches. If you come upon a beautiful woman in a snowstorm, beware! She puts travelers to sleep. Later, when they are found, they have frozen to death. Some yamauba can be good, as was the mother of Kintaro, a famous Japanese hero. She brought him up in the mountains.

Spirits that live in creeks, streams, ponds, and lakes are called *kappa*. Small as a child but very ugly, they have green skin and ducklike webs between their toes and fingers. They also have a very strange hollow spot that looks like a cup on the top of their heads. If the water that collects in this hollow spot spills out, kappa lose their strength and can be overcome.

Kappa are very bad creatures. In the evening they are said to slip out from a pond or stream and steal food from a farmer's garden. They especially like cucumbers. Kappa are also said to pull men, women, children, and horses into a river or lake in order to drown them.

Besides making up stories about creatures like the kappa, the Japanese tell many tales about *kami*, the gods of the Shinto religion. There are kami in mountains, trees, and rivers, as well as for harvests, peace, and health.

A Shinto legend says that the first kami came into being shortly after the world began. In this legend, the world was first in the form of an egg. This egg separated, with its white part becoming heaven and its yolk becoming earth. Following the separation, a reed shoot grew up between the two parts of the egg. The first kami, parent of all the other Shinto gods, sprang out of this shoot.

According to the Shinto religion, the god Izanagi and the goddess Izanami created land from droplets of water. They were also the parents of beautiful

Japanese folklore is filled with tales of strange beings. These men have dressed as devils or evil spirits for a ceremony that is part of the Namahage Festival.

Amaterasu, the sun goddess, and fierce-tempered Susano, the storm god. Amaterasu is held to be the ancestor of the emperor.

Susano once made Amaterasu very, very angry. He let wild colts loose in her rice fields, and they trampled down the precious growing rice. Amaterasu was so angry that she shut herself up in a cave in heaven and would not come out. Then the world was always dark, and nothing would grow.

The other gods and goddesses thought of a plan to make Amaterasu come out. They made a mirror and hung it from a tree in front of the cave. Then they made a lot of noise, playing music and dancing. The noise sounded as if they were having a lively party, and the more Amaterasu listened, the more she wanted to leave the cave and join them. Finally Sarume, the monkey woman, did such a funny dance, and everyone laughed so hard that Amaterasu just had to come out.

"I'll just take a peek," she said to herself.

When she looked out, she was startled to see herself in the mirror that had been hung outside the cave. The other gods and goddesses quickly took advantage of her surprise, pulling her forth and begging her not to hide any longer.

Amaterasu was persuaded by what they said, and she promised to leave her cave. Once again the sun shone, and day followed night. The mirror had done the trick. In time it became one of the most important signs of the emperor's family.

Many Japanese stories concern the gods and goddesses. Other stories are about heroes, those special people who are remembered for their great deeds. A hero's story will be told over and over. The more it is told, however, the more it begins to change. Sometimes the hero's deeds are made to appear much greater than they actually were.

Yoshitsune is a hero who became more noble in stories than he probably was in real life. In many of these stories he is accompanied by his big, strong friend Benkei, who was a monk at Mount Hiei, a Buddhist temple on the outskirts of Kyoto. Mount Hiei was famous for its fighting priests, and Benkei was one of them.

Yoshitsune and Benkei were not always friends. In fact, on the night they first met, they were both crossing Gojo Bridge in Kyoto, and Benkei challenged the young Yoshitsune to a fight. Benkei was much larger and stronger than Yoshitsune, but the young warrior won the fight. Benkei later offered to serve as one of Yoshitsune's men, and they became close friends.

The story of this fight is much like the English legend about Little John and Robin Hood. In that legend, seven-foot-tall Little John knocks Robin off a narrow bridge into a rushing stream. Each man realizes the other has put up a good fight, though, and they become good friends.

Another hero in Japanese legends is Issunboshi, a character like Tom Thumb. Although Issunboshi's parents were the same size as most Japanese, he was very tiny. When he was fifteen, he decided to go to Kyoto, the capital, to make his fortune. His parents gave him a rice bowl, a pair of chopsticks, and a needle.

Issunboshi floated down to Kyoto in the rice bowl, steering with the chopsticks. The needle was stuck in his belt as a sword.

In Kyoto, Issunboshi found work with a wealthy family. One day a wicked oni threatened the family's daughter. Tiny Issunboshi challenged the devil, and with the help of his little sword he saved the daughter's life. Then he took the oni's special hammer and made a wish to become the size of most other Japanese. Wishing on the hammer worked. Issunboshi became as tall as a man and married the princess, and they lived happily together for the rest of their lives.

The Japanese are also fond of fairy tales, stories somewhat different from legends. Fairy tales are generally longer than legends, and they deal mainly with magical beings and events. In addition, they are usually written stories, while legends are often spoken ones.

Momotaro is a fairy tale hero. In his story, an old couple wanted a child very badly. They found a large peach floating down the stream near their home. When they split it open, they discovered a child inside. The old couple named the little boy Momotaro, which means "Peach Boy."

Momotaro grew up to save his parents and their neighbors from a wicked oni. He was helped by a dog, a pheasant, and a monkey, whom he befriended on his travels. He came home a rich man, and he supported his parents for the rest of their lives.

The Japanese believe that everyone needs fairy tales and legends. For many years they have told stories about goblins, gods, and heroes. Some of these stories have been lost or forgotten, but many live on because they make Japan such a special place to its people.

5. A Festival for Everyone

Can you imagine a world without holidays? Neither can the Japanese. They hold festivals for boys and girls, ancestors and emperors, crops and fishing.

So many different kinds of holidays and festivals are celebrated in Japan that you could easily go to a different one every day of the year. Some are national holidays, like the emperor's birthday and Children's Day, while others are local festivals for neighborhood shrines or kami. Farmers hold festivals to help the rice crop, and fishermen to have good fishing.

The Japanese have also borrowed festivals from many other places. They celebrate Christmas with a special cake and sometimes with a party. Except for the Japanese Christians, however, Christmas is not a holiday of deep meaning to the Japanese. They don't even take a day off from work for it. Many labor unions have a big parade on May 1 to celebrate the Russian Revolution.

On May 5 there is a special celebration for Japanese boys and girls. Known as Children's Day, it is a national holiday. This festival was once known as Boy's Day, and many people still think of it that way. The Japanese decided to honor all children on May 5 after World War II, although they have kept a celebration for girls in March. This Girl's Day is not a national holiday.

If you are in Japan on Children's Day, you see *koinobori* flying bravely in the wind. Koinobori are huge fish made of paper or cloth. They are hung from the edge of the house or raised on a flagpole. They look like the airsocks you see at small airports. Each boy in the family has a fish flag of his own. The oldest

Koinobori, huge fish flags made of paper or cloth, are flown by Japanese boys on Children's Day (May 5).

boy in the family gets the biggest flag, and the youngest gets the smallest.

The paper fish are models of a kind of carp. Somewhat like catfish, these carp are hard fighters that have to battle their way upstream against strong currents. In the old days, the Japanese wanted their boys to become strong warriors. They thought these fish were a good sign, or symbol, for the boys.

Nowadays May 5 is a day for family outings. The trains are packed with people trying to get out of the city for a picnic or a visit to grandparents.

Girl's Day is March 3. On this day, girls all over Japan get out the special dolls that have been passed down to them from their mothers. Because these dolls are fairly old, they have been wrapped up and carefully stored away since the last Girl's Day.

After unwrapping the dolls, the girls place them on a special set of shelves. At the top are the emperor and empress dolls. These two rule over the other dolls—servants, guards, musicians, and courtiers. At the bottom, the girls place tiny furniture or musical instruments. Rice cakes called *hisimochi* are also put on the shelves.

Girl's Day comes from a much older Shinto celebration welcoming spring. Years ago on this day, the Japanese rubbed their bodies with small paper dolls. Then they threw the dolls into a river or stream. They believed that the evil spirits from winter went into the dolls and were washed away by the water.

On March 3, Girl's Day, girls from all over Japan display ceremonial dolls on a special set of shelves. These dolls have often been passed down from mothers to daughters for many generations.

Several other festivals are held for children. *Shichi-go-san* ("seven-five-three") takes place on November 15. It is for three-year-old boys and girls, five-year-old girls, and seven-year-old boys. The children are dressed in their best clothes. They go to the shrine with their parents and grandparents, who pray for the children's health. The youngsters also get presents.

On Shichi-go-san Day, seven, five, and three-year-old children dress in traditional costumes and visit a shrine with their families to offer prayers for health and good fortune.

On July 7, the Weaver Star and the Shepherd Star meet in the Milky Way. According to a Chinese legend, these stars can grant children wishes. The legend came to Japan centuries ago as the *Tanabata* Festival.

To celebrate the Tanabata Festival, Japanese children make decorations to put on a bamboo branch. Their parents help them carve little animals from vegetables. They make paper chains, too. Then they write their wishes on little strips of paper and tie the strips to the bamboo branch. According to tradition, wishes should only be written with ink made from morning dew. In the evening, the children throw the decorated bamboo branch into a stream or pond.

Besides having their own special celebrations, Japanese children take part in other festivals. On *O-shōgatsu*, the biggest festival of the year in Japan, they bow and smile after greeting friends with the words *Akemashite omedetoo gozaimasu* ("Happy New Year"). At one time everyone became a year older at New Year's. That made O-shogatsu like a big birthday party for all the Japanese people. Today each person celebrates his or her own birthday.

New Year's in Japan is a Shinto festival of new life and cleansing. At first it was a fifteen-day celebration, like the twelve days of Christmas or the eight days of Hanukkah. Now it takes place mainly on New Year's Eve and New Year's Day.

By the time New Year's Eve comes, the family has put up New Year's decorations outside the house. These decorations are made of pine and bamboo. They also include a special rope that stands for the one the gods used to close off the cave in which Amaterasu, the sun goddess, had hidden.

A special cake made of pounded rice is placed in the tokonoma of the living room. Big, flat, and pure white, it is called *kagami mochi*, or mirror cake. The cake stands for the mirror that Amaterasu looked into when she peeked out of her cave.

New Year's Eve is a busy time. Everyone is cleaning house. All the food needed for New Year's has to be cooked before midnight because, by custom, no cooking is allowed the next day. New Year's Eve is also the day for people to pay all their old debts.

The last meal of the old year is *soba*, or buckwheat noodles. Later in the evening, the Japanese might watch "Koohaku Utagasen." This yearly "song battle of Red against White" is a contest featuring Japanese singing stars—men on a white team and women on a red one.

During the contest, single performers or groups on each team sing music that is popular in Japan—folksongs, Bing Crosby tunes, pop hits. They are awarded points for their effort by a panel of ten to twelve celebrity judges. The singers also earn points for the number of favorable calls listeners phone in to the station after their performance. At the end of the program, the team with the most points wins the contest.

At midnight the big bells of the temples ring out joyously to celebrate the New Year. Families go to the temples to pray for luck in the year to come.

Because New Year's Day is a Shinto festival of cleansing, people go to a public bath early the next morning. Ordinarily the baths do not open until 4:00 P.M., but they are open by 8:00 A.M. on New Year's, the only day of the year the Japanese bathe in the morning. After bathing, everyone puts on clean clothing and returns home.

At the first meal of the New Year, families drink *o-tosu*, sweet spiced wine. They also have a soup called *o-zoni*, along with many other traditional dishes. The children receive presents of money in special, pretty envelopes.

On New Year's morning the mail carrier delivers all the New Year's cards. Can you imagine all your Christmas cards arriving in a stack on Christmas Day? Japanese families read their greeting cards as they eat breakfast or relax.

In the afternoon many visits are made to friends or relatives to wish them a "Happy New Year." Gifts are also exchanged. Girls play a traditional game that is like badminton, and boys take their kites out to fly.

Many people like to play a very old card game called *utakaruta*. Instead of being printed with hearts, spades, clubs, or diamonds, each card contains part of a poem from a famous collection of one hundred poems called the *Hyakuinshu*. The object of the game is to match the two halves of the poems correctly.

The Shinto celebration for the New Year is the biggest festival of the year. Another important time is *Obon*, a Buddhist festival for the spirits of the dead that is held in the summer.

During Obon, Japanese families welcome back the spirits of their ancestors. Most villages in Japan celebrate Obon in mid-July, but some celebrate later. Kyoto has a big celebration in the middle of August.

On the first day of the festival, people clean their houses from top to bottom. Then they lay tablets showing the names of their ancestors in front of the family altar.

When the work in the house is done, people clean and decorate their ancestors' graves. In the evening they return to the graveyard, carrying lanterns to lead the ancestors' spirits back home with them. These spirits are believed to stay in the house until the last night of Obon.

On the last night of the Obon festival rice dumplings called *dango* are served for dinner. Then the family says good-bye to the spirits and lights their way back to the graveyard with a lantern or a fire. In Kyoto huge fires are lit at several locations around the city. Some people put paper lanterns in a toy boat and float it down a stream.

Bon odori, a dance that both young and old take part in, is one of the most exciting parts of the Obon festival. Driven by a loud drum and a singer's voice, everyone dances for hours in a big circle. Some wear kimonos, while others wear jeans.

In almost all Japanese festivals, some kind of rice is eaten. Kagami mochi is served for New Year's, and hisimochi for Girl's Day. Rice cakes wrapped in oak leaves are eaten on Children's Day, and dango on the last night of Obon. In the old days, rice was not only grown for food but was also used as money. Rice paid the rent and the taxes.

Not surprisingly then, Japan has many rice festivals. They are performed yearly following the growing seasons. One of the biggest rice festivals is held in spring, when young rice is moved from seedling beds into flooded paddies where it will grow until harvest time.

As they replant the rice, workers sing traditional songs, stepping and bending together to the beat of a drum. The songs make the hard work go faster.

In the summer, there is a festival for the wind god. He is asked to protect the rice from the typhoons. In September or October there is even a festival for the scarecrows, when they are pulled up for the year after the harvest.

The rice festivals, like those for children, ancestors, and the new year, are very important to the Japanese. Besides being times for rest and celebration, they bring families and friends together. Most of all, festivals help people to express their beliefs and feelings about the meaning of birth, life, and death.

6. Home: A Warm, Safe Place

Most Japanese live in small houses or apartments located in noisy city neighborhoods. Can you imagine the sounds you would hear on a street outside a home in Osaka, Kyoto, or Tokyo?

One sound is the recorded message that often drones from a loudspeaker mounted on top of a small pickup truck: "Please recycle your old newspapers and magazines." Recycling is necessary because Japan has to buy much of its lumber and paper from other countries. Most people are willing to save paper because they know it will be regularly collected.

Another sound comes from a small hand horn. "Waaanh, waaanh," it beeps, as a foodseller pushing an aluminum cart starts down the street.

When the horn sounds, a mother slips into *geta*, wooden sandals. "Clip-clap, clip-clap" go the shoes as she hurries out to meet the *tofu* seller. Opening the top of his cart, he reaches into a water-filled container, and pulls out a palm-size block of white tofu, soybean curd. Then he ties it in a bag for her so that she can carry it home.

As the woman pays for the tofu, she and the seller hear a rhythmic beat coming from the back of a house. "Whack, whack, whack," pause, "thud, thud, thud." Another mother is knocking the dust out of her family's bedding, bright quilts called *futon*, with a beater made of bamboo and palm stem.

Just as the mother finishes with the futon, a large green tank truck drives up to her house. The driver climbs out, runs a hose from the truck to a tank in her yard, and turns on a pump. "Whir, whoosh, gurgle," the pump cleans out the family's septic tank.

Many Japanese homes do not have flush toilets, and wastes must be transferred to a septic tank. About every two weeks a truck comes by and cleans the tank out. The waste is sold to farmers, who use it for fertilizer.

His work done, the driver moves on to another house on another street. As he leaves, an older man and woman are about to enter their house. A sliding door lets them into the *genkan*, the entrance way.

Every Japanese home has some kind of genkan that separates it from the outside. In an apartment the genkan may be no more than a small space; in an old farmhouse, it may be as wide as a room. No matter what its size, though, the genkan has a pleasant, cool feeling. Once you enter it, you know that you have left the street behind.

From the genkan, a step leads up to the main part of the house. Here you will usually notice several pairs of shoes. Each pair has been turned so that its owner can step into the shoes with no trouble when leaving.

The inside of a traditional Japanese house is carpeted with *tatami*, thick mats of rice straw. Tatami has been used for a very long time. In fact, rooms are measured by the size of the mats—a 3-mat room, a 6-mat room, and so on.

The Japanese never wear shoes on tatami. If the house has rooms with wooden floors, they sometimes wear slippers. But when they enter a tatami-covered

Straw mats, called tatami, cover the floors of a traditional Japanese house. They are very comfortable to sleep on, especially when you are lying inside a thick, quiltlike futon.

room, they take the slippers off. Separate slippers are used in the bathroom because the Japanese are concerned about cleanliness.

Many families live in just one or two rooms. The dining room, living room, and bedrooms are all combined into one. Since tatami is comfortable to sit on, there is no need for chairs, which would take up space. Tatami is also comfortable to sleep on, especially when you're wrapped in a thick futon. The quiltlike futon can be folded up and stored in a closet during the day to make more room for the family.

Because their living area is so small, the Japanese center their homes around one low table in the middle of the room. Americans can place sofas, chairs, and desks against the walls of a room because they have more space than the Japanese.

Most Americans can also bathe in their own homes. In Japan, however, many homes don't have private baths, although more and more families are putting them in. To keep clean, the Japanese use public baths, which are easy to find because they always have a dark blue curtain hanging out front. The curtain displays the hiragana symbol *yu*, which means hot water.

At public baths, men and boys dress and bathe in one area, women and girls in another. The bathers each bring a plastic wash basin, soap, and a long

Because Japanese homes are quite small, they are centered around one small table in the middle of the living area.

washcloth. After they have undressed, they slide open a glass door and enter a hot, steamy room.

This tiled room has a big, deep tub, somewhat like a small swimming pool. The tub is filled with very, very hot water. Around the edge of the room is a low row of faucets used for washing. People splash water over themselves with the basin, and then begin to scrub with soap and washcloth. And the Japanese really do scrub!

After they have rinsed off all the soap, the Japanese get into the tub. They think that washing in the tub is dirty, and they will not enter it until they are clean. Then they soak for as long as they can stand the hot water. Sometimes people like to splash themselves with cold water after they are done soaking.

Rather than drying off with a big, fluffy towel, the Japanese wring out their washcloths and use them to wipe the water off their bodies. Coming out of the steamy bath into the cooler dressing area also helps them to dry off.

Whenever someone leaves home to use a public bath, or to go to work or school, the Japanese use special phrases. In the morning, for example, a mother will sing out, *Itte irasshai* ("See you later!"), as her child leaves the house. The child will reply, *Itte kimasu* ("Yes. See you in a while."). In the afternoon, a child returning home will say, *Tadaima* ("Hey! I'm home."). The mother will answer, *Okaeri* ("Welcome home.").

In many Japanese homes, grandparents answer *Okaeri* to *Tadaima*. Grandparents are very important members of the family. They stay at home and watch the house when everyone else leaves, which is one reason there is little robbery in Japan. They also care for babies and tell stories to anyone who has time to listen.

The grandparents like to be at home. They can enjoy their grandchildren, meet and talk with friends, and be a part of their community. Few of them really want to live by themselves or in a rest home. Only about half of Japan's old people live with their children, though. Many children say they don't have the room or the time to care for their aged parents.

Old people who do live with their children sometimes go with the mother when she walks to the market to do her daily shopping. She shops each day because the Japanese like to cook with food that is as fresh as possible. In addition, most Japanese homes don't have big freezers or refrigerators for storing food.

"Welcome, welcome," call out the stall owners in the market where the mother shops. They have many interesting foods for sale. One seller's stall is filled with pickled vegetables. Barrels and buckets of eggplants, radishes, mustard greens, and Chinese cabbages are displayed. Next to this seller's stall a family is selling *miso*. Miso looks like dark peanut butter, but it is made from fermented soybeans and is used in soup.

Other sellers have eggs or treats for sale. In Japan eggs are bought one-by-one, not by the dozen. The egg seller picks them out and wraps them in a sheet of newspaper. Among the treats is a fish-shaped waffle

Japanese mothers make daily shopping trips to the market because they like to cook with fresh food.

filled with sweet bean paste. It is made fresh at the market. Shoppers can also buy animal crackers or candy.

In most countries working women have little time for cooking. They may eat breakfast on a coffee break or go out to lunch with friends. Sometimes they are too tired to fix dinner, and they take the family out to eat.

In Japan most women must spend time shopping and cooking every day. Many Japanese mothers may soon become like other working women, though, because half of them are going back to work after their youngest child enters school. Perhaps they will also take their families out to eat once in a while.

Japanese girls learn cooking from their mothers. Cooking schools are very popular, too. Japanese boys, however, are seldom allowed to do anything in the kitchen. Many young men go off to college without even knowing how to turn on a kitchen stove.

Although families usually eat home-cooked meals, Japanese houses are too small to invite many people for dinners or parties. Only close friends are entertained at home. People in business do not ask their bosses or other workers to come to their homes for dinner. Instead, they take their guests to a restaurant and afterwards go to a club for drinks.

Both managers and workers put in long hours on

their jobs, sometimes working six days a week. They want to earn enough money to send their children to the best schools. Japanese mothers often give up their jobs and outside interests in order to stay at home. They want to be there to guide and teach their children.

Most Japanese children have an easy, carefree life at home until they start school at age six. In fact, they are hardly ever scolded. For example, they can burst into a conversation between their father and his friends without anyone saying, "Please don't interrupt." Once children enter school, however, they are expected to act in the Japanese way. No one laughs if they forget to speak properly and be polite.

The Japanese believe that the parents are at fault if a child has problems. In Japan the family must accept the blame when a child does something wrong.

The many ways in which parents help their children show Japanese youngsters how much they are loved. In return, the children usually respect their parents and care for them in their old age. *On* is the special word for this feeling of love and responsibility.

Because children can depend on their families, Japan is a warm, safe place for them to grow up in. Mothers, fathers, grandparents, and friends are always there to help. But in turn each person is expected to give much of his or her life to the family.

Most Japanese children have a happy, secure homelife.

Many young people in Japan today feel that they are asked to give too much of their lives to their families. They want to make more decisions for themselves—decisions about friends, marriage, and jobs. Some young people would rather not have their parents move in with them when the father retires.

Other young people cannot care for their parents because more and more women with families are working. All of these women want to be paid as much as men for doing the same work. They also want to be respected as much as men. In Japanese businesses, women earn less money than men, and they are not given a chance to do the more important jobs. But since more women in Japan are returning to work, businesses may begin to give them better jobs and fairer pay.

How children's lives will change as more mothers begin working is difficult to say. Perhaps they will grow closer to their fathers. Possibly they will have to become more helpful around the house. Certainly they will wish that their mothers had more time to spend with them.

Yet whatever changes occur, the children will be well cared for. Their parents will work hard to give them a good home and a good education. For though the world may change, homes and families will always be important to the Japanese.

The Japanese are famous for their tasty dishes. Here are three recipes you may want to try.

Oyako Domburi
Oyako means parent and child. In this case it refers to the chicken and the egg. Oyako domburi is chicken and egg over rice. A very common meal, it is served in many inexpensive restaurants, and daily in many people's homes.
To make this recipe you need:

1 pound of raw chicken cut into bite-size pieces (buy it
    boned or bone a chicken breast)
1-1/3 cups mushrooms, sliced thin (fresh, not canned)
1 cup onions, sliced into crescents
1/2 cup plus 2 tablespoons chicken stock
1/4 cup cooking sherry or *sake* (rice wine)
2 tablespoons soy sauce
4 cups cooked rice (white or brown)
4 eggs
cooking oil
saucepan
small frying pan
spatula

Steps in the Recipe
1. Cut up the chicken and divide it into four 1/4

pound portions.

2. Slice the mushrooms and the onions. Cut each onion slice in half to make crescents.
3. Using the saucepan, make the sauce by combining the following:

    1/2 cup plus 2 tablespoons chicken stock
    1/4 cup cooking sherry or sake
    2 tablespoons soy sauce (use more if you like a stronger taste)

4. Cook four cups of rice.
5. Pour a tiny amount of cooking oil into a small frying pan.
6. Using a medium heat, add 1/4 cup of the onions and sauté until clear. Then add 1/4 pound of the chicken and 1/3 cup of the mushrooms and stir, cooking until the chicken is partially done — about 5 minutes.
7. Lower heat slightly. Add 1/4 cup of the sauce to the vegetables in the frying pan. Cook the sauce and the vegetables for about 30 seconds.
8. Pour 1 lightly beaten egg over the sauce and the vegetables. Cover the frying pan and cook until the egg has set.
9. Using a spatula, slide omelette with sauce over 1 cup cooked rice.
10. Repeat steps 5-10 three more times to make a total of four servings.

Okonomiyaki

When the Japanese want to eat a simple but filling food, they often make vegetable pancakes called okonomiyaki. One large pancake is considered a serving. Two large pancakes can be prepared from this recipe.

To make this recipe you need:

1/2 cup chopped onion
1 cup chopped cabbage
1 grated carrot
1 cup white flour
1 pinch salt
1/8 teaspoon baking soda
1 egg
3/4 cup milk
2 teaspoons soy sauce
1/2 teaspoon sugar
1 tablespoon cooking oil
small frying pan
large mixing bowl
medium frying pan
spatula

You can vary the recipe by using other vegetables: green peppers, green onions, bok choy, parsley, or icicle radishes. For seasonings you might add sesame oil, ginger, or small portions of diced pickles. (Japanese pickles would be best.) Some people prefer to use whole wheat flour instead of white flour. The whole wheat flour will make a heavier, stickier pancake.

Steps in the Recipe
1. Chop the onions and cabbage, and grate the carrots.
2. Using low heat, brown these vegetables in a tiny amount of cooking oil in a small frying pan.
3. Make the pancake batter by mixing the flour, salt, baking soda, egg, milk, soy sauce, and sugar together in a large bowl.
4. Mix the lightly-browned vegetables into the batter.
5. Lightly cover the bottom of a medium-size frying pan with cooking oil.
6. Pour enough batter into the frying pan to make 1 large 6-inch pancake.
7. Cook the pancake until one side is brown. Then flip it with the spatula and cook the other side.
8. Remove the cooked pancake and keep it hot until it is served.
9. Repeat steps 6-8 to make the second pancake.

Okonomiyaki should be served hot. Some people like to put soy sauce on them.

Tempura

Tempura is the Japanese dish best known to Westerners. It is actually a variation of Portugese cooking, borrowed from missionaries who came to Japan in 1600. Until that time the Japanese had very few fried dishes, probably because they had very few sources of cooking oil.

To make this recipe you need:
Several kinds of vegetables—green peppers, green beans, carrots, mushrooms, onion slices, summer squash or zucchini, sweet potatoes, eggplants
1/2 cup *dashi* (Japanese soup stock) or chicken broth
3 tablespoons soy sauce
1/4 cup cooking sherry or sake (rice wine)
1 lemon
grated white radish or scallions
water
flour
1 egg
saucepan
small frying pan
cooking oil
cooked rice
spatula
2 mixing bowls (one larger than the other)

Steps in the Recipe

1. Prepare the vegetables for frying. Use enough vegetables so that each person can try several kinds. Cut green peppers in long slices, and carrots in long and thin slices. Cut mushrooms in half. Japanese eggplants should be sliced in half, lengthways. Standard eggplants should be cut into 1/2 inch slices, and each slice should be cut into four parts.

2. Using the saucepan, make the sauce by combining the following:

    > 1/2 cup dashi (Japanese soup stock) or chicken broth
    >
    > 3 tablespoons soy sauce
    >
    > 1/4 cup cooking sherry or sake (rice wine)
    >
    > 1 good squeeze of lemon

    Put out grated white radishes or chopped scallions that can be added to this sauce. Serve the sauce warm in small bowls when the tempura is ready.

3. Get the bowls ready to make the batter. Tempura lovers insist that the batter should be made in small amounts, and that it should be kept as cold as possible. I try to do both things by using two bowls, one larger than the other. I place a layer of ice cubes in the larger bowl and set the smaller one on top of them. Then I mix the batter in the smaller bowl. When I make large amounts of tem-

pura, I often make several batches of batter.

4. Make the batter. Begin by adding 1/4 cup of water and 1 lightly beaten egg to 1/2 cup of flour. Mix them together and add more water if the flour remains powdery. The mixture should look and feel like a thick pancake batter.

5. Fill a small frying pan with about 1 inch of vegetable oil. Warm the oil, using low heat.

6. Test the heat of the oil by dropping a small bit of batter into it. The batter should fall to the bottom, be immediately surrounded by bubbles, and then rise quickly to the top. If this does not happen quickly, the oil is not hot enough for cooking. Be careful not to let the oil burn, or the tempura will have a bad flavor.

7. Dip the vegetables in the batter, covering them completely. Then drop the vegetables into the oil.

8. Turn the vegetables once, but don't wait until their coating of batter turns brown, or they will be overcooked.

9. Take the vegetables out of the pan when they are crisp. Place them on paper towels so that the oil can drain off. Use the oven to keep the tempura warm until they are served.

Tempura should be served with a side dish of cooked rice.

As you can see, the Japanese eat a lot of rice and vegetables. Fish, soybean curd and paste, and seaweed are also important foods in their diet, along with meat and dairy products.

You might want to try eating these recipes with chopsticks. These slender, wooden, tapered sticks serve as forks in Japan and other Asian nations.

The basic idea in using chopsticks is to pinch a piece of food between the two sticks so that you can pick it up. To do this, you should hold one stick steady and move the other one. Here are the two essential steps:

1. Hold one stick between the base of your thumb and your fourth finger. Keep this stick still.
2. Hold the other stick by your thumb and your second and third fingers. Move this stick.

There are two other things you should remember. If you hold the chopsticks too close to the ends that pick up the food, you can't easily pinch them together. If you hold them too tight, you'll get a cramp.

With a little practice, you'll find that it's really not hard to use chopsticks, and I'm sure you'll find them fun to try.

7. School Days

Cherry blossoms are in bloom, and paper, notebooks, and pencil boxes go on display in stores. Then one fine spring day, children are back at their desks. In Japan the new school year starts in April.

Doing well in school is very important to the Japanese. Students must pass difficult tests to get into high school and college. Some students must even take tests to enter junior high school.

Children and their parents do not expect school to be easy. Having to study hard seems as natural and right to them as eating rice or drinking green tea.

Because school is so important, Japanese children have less vacation time from school than children in other countries. They are given three main breaks from their studies. Summer vacation is about forty days long, from July 20 to the end of August. Another vacation takes place at New Year's time, from December 24 to January 8. In the spring, schools are closed from March 20 to the end of the first week in April. Then the new school year begins.

Japanese children also go to school more days each week than some youngsters. From Monday to Friday they are in school until about three in the

Although Japanese students have a long schoolweek, not all of their time is spent in the classroom. These students are working on a nature project.

afternoon. On Saturdays they go to school from eight in the morning until noon.

In Japan, as in other lands, some children like school, and some don't. Likewise, some children do well in school, while others have problems no matter how hard they try.

Japanese mothers and fathers want their children to be good students, and most are happy if the children do their best. However, some mothers push their children very, very hard to do well in school. They are called *kyoiku mama*, which means "education mama." A kyoiku mama drills her children like a teacher. Sometimes she even sharpens her children's pencils.

Since World War II, the Japanese school system has been the same as the American one. The American government helped build the new system after Japan's defeat in the war. Beginning at age six, Japanese children go to elementary school for grades one through six. Then they attend a junior high school for seventh, eighth, and ninth grades, and a high school for grades ten, eleven, and twelve. Children must stay in school through ninth grade, but few of them drop out or fail to pass the tests for entering high school.

The government in Tokyo determines what subjects the children must learn, whether they live in Kyushu, Shikoku, Honshu, or Hokkaido. In the United States, this decision is made by the individual states and school districts. Each local school in Japan is allowed to decide how its students will be taught and what textbooks they will use. The National Ministry of Education must approve the textbooks.

In grade school, students study the same things you do—reading, writing, and arithmetic. To be able to write they must know hiragana, katakana, and Chinese characters. They have to spend many hours learning the thousands of characters.

Students of all ages must study math. They begin with arithmetic and move on to algebra, geometry, and advanced mathematics. Because so much time is spent on math, Japanese students in grades seven to twelve learn it more quickly than American students in the same grades.

As they get older, Japanese children add more difficult classes to their schedule. In most of their classes they need to memorize facts, names, and terms. They take Japanese literature, Japanese history, world history, geography, science, and English.

Art classes are an important part of school. In spring grade school students often go outside to draw pictures of trees, plants, birds, and insects. *Origami*, paper folding, is taught in the classroom. Teachers feel that origami helps children learn to use their fingers and to improve their math skills.

Art is one of the important classes in Japanese grade schools.
These happy students are sketching a harbor scene.

Japanese children, like children everywhere, look forward most to the times when they can play with their friends. During school friends can see each other three times a week in physical education class. After school they can play together in swimming, track, music, or softball clubs. Volleyball and ping-pong clubs are also very popular.

Physical education is given great emphasis in Japanese schools today.

The big school field trip gives children another chance to have fun with friends. On these trips, which last for two or three days, students visit important historic places in Japan. They see where the history they have been studying really happened. The older the students are, the farther they travel.

For all students the field trips come at the end of elementary school, junior high school, and the eleventh grade. The third big trip is held at the end of eleventh grade, rather than twelfth grade, because twelfth graders cannot take time off for a trip. They are studying hard to pass their college entrance tests.

During March busload after busload of students travels to famous shrines and temples. Some students visit Tokyo, where the Japanese Diet meets, and where the emperor's palace is located. Others go to Kyoto or Nara, where there are many palaces and shrines. Still others visit Ise, the home of the Imperial Shrine, the shrine of the emperor's family.

The students stay in hostels, shelters for young people, and in special centers set up for student travelers. In their free time they roam the shopping streets of the city with their friends. They buy small gifts for their families and take many photographs of each other.

Most Japanese remember their school trips as one of the best times of their lives. They fondly recall

*One of the famous places that students visit on their school
trips is Himeji Castle in Hyogo Prefecture. Completed in 1609,
it is said to have taken nine years to build.*

the fun they had shopping, talking, and laughing with their friends.

Almost all students in Japan take extra classes after school. Many sign up for a special class in English. Japanese children start studying English in seventh grade, but some begin earlier by taking private classes or working on their own to prepare for tests.

The Japanese must know English because it is the common language of businesses throughout the world. A man or woman needs to understand English to work in most Japanese companies.

Soroban is another class that many children take after school. Soroban is the Japanese name for the Chinese abacus, a simple, hand-operated computer discovered by the Chinese thousands of years ago. The four sides of the soroban hold round wooden bead markers strung on rods. These bead markers are used for counting. For some Japanese, using the soroban is as fast as using an electronic calculator.

In Japan numbers are written in arabic numerals—1, 2, 3, and so forth. The Japanese can also write their numbers with Chinese characters. However, arabic numerals are easier to use in modern math.

Some children have private tutors, people who teach them in their homes. Parents often hire a uni-

These students are learning to use the soroban, a simple, wooden, hand-operated computer.

versity student as a tutor for their high-school-age son or daughter. Usually, they try to hire a student at the school their child wants to enter. Some parents even hire a professor from the university as a tutor!

Japanese grade school children spend one to two hours every day doing homework. Yet they also watch a lot of television—two and one-half hours daily.

Children in Japan also like to read books after school, especially comic books. We think of a comic book as a slim, one adventure magazine. In Japan it is a fat book with many different stories and articles. Although this comic book costs three or four times more than the thinner one, it is well worth the money.

Few young people in Japan have jobs after school. Their parents would rather have them spend their free time studying.

The race to get a good education starts early in Japanese schools. Most parents want their children to go to a good grade school, because students who do well there usually get into a good junior high school. Some children take tests to enter a top private kindergarten. Their parents believe this kind of kindergarten will best prepare them for grade school.

For most children the pressure to do well starts late in grade school. As they pass from one grade to the next, they have to work harder and harder at their studies. In twelfth grade they study day and night to pass the tests for entering college. Instead of spending one or two hours on homework, they stay up long after midnight. Sometimes they drink strong coffee to help keep themselves awake. They give up watching TV and reading books for fun. Studying also leaves little time for friends. Besides, all the students and their friends can talk about are the upcoming tests. And they all know the same thing: the hardest schools to enter give the most difficult tests.

Students who are not sure that studying, tutors, and afterschool classes will get them into a certain school may ask the gods for help. Many of them go to Kitano Shrine in Kyoto. Built in honor of a Heian period scholar, this place of worship has become special to all students. Every year thousands of them visit the shrine and pray for good luck on their tests. They hope the gods will reward them for their hard work.

The students know, of course, that they must think carefully and remember what they have studied to do well on their tests. Yet they are willing to try prayer because a good education is so highly valued in Japan.

8. Sports: Old and New

In 1964 the Olympic Games were held in Tokyo. Never before had they taken place in Japan or in any other part of Asia. The Japanese worked hard to have Tokyo chosen as the site of the Olympics and to get everything ready for the visiting athletes.

Having the Olympic Games in Tokyo meant a great deal to the Japanese. After their defeat in World War II, they felt that Western nations had lost respect for them. Now they thought that people in Europe and North America were willing to treat them as equals.

At the 1964 games, the Japanese women's volleyball team won the gold medal. Volleyball is the most popular women's sport in Japan, and girls spend hours playing it. The twelve women on the Olympic volleyball team, all office clerks or factory workers, practiced eight hours a day—after work!

During their long practices, the Japanese women learned a new skill that enabled them to defeat a taller Russian team. Their coach taught them how to reach shots that used to hit the floor just beyond their outstretched hands. They spent hours learning how to fall to the floor, to somersault, and to come up on

The Olympic Games were held in Tokyo in 1964, marking the first time this major sports festival was staged in an Asian nation.

their feet ready to hit the ball again. All of them forgot about their aching muscles and bruised knees when they won the gold medal, though.

Having their teams do well at the 1964 Olympics

*These junior high school girls are learning to play volleyball,
Japan's most popular women's sport, in physical education
class.*

was important to the Japanese. They wanted to show
the world that their athletes could compete on an
international level. Japanese athletes have also won
Olympic medals in judo, wrestling, and gymnastics.

Japanese children begin playing sports in grade school. They have a physical education class two or three times a week all through their school years. In this class they play ball games, practice tumbling, run races, and high jump. If their school has a swimming pool, they take swimming classes.

Physical education teachers also use their classes to teach children to follow orders. They use drills in which the children learn to line up straight, or run, stop, and turn on command.

Like volleyball, many sports in Japan are played around the world. *Sumo*, though, is a Japanese sport seldom found outside of Japan. Perhaps you've seen pictures of sumo wrestlers. They are quite fat, and their hair is tied up high in a top knot. This hairstyle becomes fancier as they earn a higher rank. Only a single white cloth wrapped around their hips covers the wrestlers' huge bodies.

Many sumo wrestlers are over six feet tall and weigh 300 pounds. The wrestlers need to be heavy because the object of sumo is to force the other wrestler out of the ring or down onto the ground.

A very old sport, sumo began during the Heian period and has been changed and refined over the centuries. Today there are six big wrestling events a year. They are held in major cities and last fifteen days.

At first a sumo match looks like the wrestlers are just going to fool around. For three or four minutes they don't grab each other. During this time they toss salt into the ring to clean its floor, and they clap their hands, throw out their arms, and stamp their feet. Each of these movements has a religious meaning. By clapping their hands, they get the attention of the gods. By throwing out their arms, they prove they have no weapons. And by stamping their feet, they beat evil forces into the ground.

Next the wrestlers bend down and place their hands on the floor. They pound the floor with their fists and give each other killing looks. The referee yells to the wrestlers. Again they pound the floor and stare angrily at each other.

The crowd senses that the match is about to begin. Everyone knows that the wrestlers have been studying each other, trying to understand how the other man will act.

Suddenly the wrestlers spring for each other. After a short struggle, one gains a hold. Then using this hold and his huge weight, he forces the other man down, quickly ending the match. There are sixty-eight holds in sumo, and when a wrestler is caught in one of them, he can lose in just a few seconds.

Sumo is a very Japanese sport. It's not part of the Olympics, and few non-Japanese have tried it. Jesse

Kuhaulua of Hawaii is one who did. In 1964, at the age of twenty, Jesse came to Japan to start his sumo training. The work was hard, as it is for all young wrestlers. But it was harder for Jesse because he was a stranger in a strange land.

Jesse lived in a dormitory with the other wrestlers. He got up at 5:00 A.M. every morning and practiced until noon—seven hours of hard work on an empty stomach. The young wrestlers weren't allowed to eat until the older wrestlers had eaten. They had to serve the older wrestlers, too. If there wasn't enough for the younger wrestlers to eat their fill, they would go hungry.

During training, a sumo wrestler's only food is *chanko*, a special dish that helps him gain weight. It's made with meat, chicken, or fish, and vegetables such as carrots, cabbage, and onions. Tofu and eggs are also added. Chanko is cooked in soy sauce and sugar. Jesse ate chanko, but he wanted American food.

Jesse trained hard, and it paid off. Now called Takamiyama, he is a grand champion sumo wrestler and a Japanese superstar, who is often seen on television.

Many Japanese boys don't think about becoming sumo wrestlers when they grow up. If they are asked what they want to be, they usually say, "a baseball player." This answer explains why boys, bats, and balls are a common sight in Japan. In schoolyards, streets, and the open spaces around a temple, you often see a group of boys playing baseball.

Girls rarely play baseball with the boys. Instead, they play softball. Girls do watch baseball games as eagerly as anyone else, though, and they keep up with the records of the great baseball stars.

Baseball is one of the most popular sports in Japan. Even high school and college games draw large crowds. An American teacher brought baseball to Japan in 1873. Later, visits by American major league teams helped to interest people in the sport. In 1936 the Tokyo Giants played their first game, and ever since then umpires have shouted "Play Ball," or *puure booru* as the Japanese say.

Many Americans laugh at the idea of Japanese baseball players. They wouldn't laugh, however, if they saw the teams in action. The Japanese are good hardball players, and their pitchers are known for their sharp curve balls.

Japanese baseball games are much like American ones. They usually last nine innings, and play can be exciting or dull, fast or slow. During the game, you can hear some familiar baseball terms. *Hitto* means hit, *sturiki* means strike, *booru* means ball, and *fouru* means foul.

Of course, Japanese and American baseball differ

Baseball was brought to Japan by an American teacher in 1873. Today it is played by schoolchildren, college students, and professionals, and is one of the country's favorite sports.

somewhat. The Japanese fields are a little smaller, and salaries are quite small compared to the huge sums paid to American players. In addition, Japanese umpires don't have as much power as American umpires. They also frequently change their calls— "Out" to "Safe," and "Ball" to "Strike." Players don't yell dirty names at the umpires, but they do push them. Umpires sometimes have to stop fights between players in order to keep the game going.

Japanese baseball has its share of superstars, too. Sadaharu Oh, a left-handed batter, is one of the greatest. Born in 1940, he joined the Tokyo Giants when he was eighteen. He was with them until he was forty, retiring at the end of the 1980 baseball season. Sadaharu Oh, or Wan-chan as his fans call him, hit 868 home runs during his years on the Giants, and he had a .301 career batting average.

Oh was known for his batting style, as well as his batting records. He stood on one leg, like a flamingo, as the ball approached, and then cracked it. And would that ball fly! At five feet, ten inches, and 180 pounds, Oh was about the size of many American players.

Japanese baseball teams also try to hire American players. A rule states that they can't have more than two foreigners on the same team at a time, though. Japanese teams often hire American players who are reaching the end of their careers in the United States. George Altman, Don Buford, Joe Stanka, and Roy White have been among these players.

Baseball is a modern team sport that has become very popular in Japan. The Japanese also like traditional fighting sports that match one player against another. In three of these sports, *judo*, *karate*, and *aikido*, players use holds and throws to win. They also need to know the strong and weak points of the human body and to keep their minds on the match.

These three sports are now taught in many countries. In America the army teaches soldiers ways to fight that are based on karate and judo. Women's self-defense classes also make use of the holds and throws of judo and aikido.

Another sport that both girls and boys study is *kendo*, Japanese fencing. They have to learn the seven basic strokes and the thrust. In kendo, as in other Japanese sports, fencers try to understand how the person they are matched against will act.

Traditional Japanese sports are played in special clothing. Kendo is played in *hakama*, old-fashioned divided skirts. The players also wear gloves, and their faces are protected by masks. The belt-tied jackets and loose pants worn by karate players are well known to North Americans. Aikido players wear hakama and a karate jacket.

Some Japanese like modern games more than traditional sports. One of their favorite games is *pachinko*, which is played on pinball machines. Players pull a lever, and a coiled spring shoots a little metal ball to the top of the game. The ball then begins to roll down, bouncing off of plastic pins and curves. To score, the ball must fall in a little hole. Some holes are worth more points than others. If the ball doesn't fall in a hole, no points are scored.

Ping, ping, ping—the silver balls shoot up and then fall down—clink, clink, clank. Pulling the lever of the pachinko machine is a daily exercise for many Japanese. It could almost be called a sport.

The Japanese are always willing to try sports played in other countries. They learn about games that are popular in other lands from their newspapers and magazines. Frisbees, jogging, and skateboarding have been brought into Japan from America.

Swimming, tennis, hiking, and rock climbing are also popular. In the winter, thousands of Japanese head for the ski slopes. The Japanese Alps in central Honshu are a paradise for skiers.

In 1970 an all-Japanese mountain climbing team reached the top of Mount Everest. It was only the sixth team that has ever climbed to the top of the world's highest mountain. In 1975 a Japanese became the first woman to reach the summit of Everest.

The Japanese Alps, located on the island of Honshu, attract thousands of mountain climbers and skiers.

The Japanese enjoy sports such as tennis, volley-ball, sumo, baseball, and kendo because they like to watch and play games with their friends. Sports also help them to let out their angry feelings, which build up from always having to be polite and proper. Through sports the Japanese can compete in a healthy and harmless way.

9. *The Japanese in the United States*

Try asking your classmates, "Where does your family come from?" You will get many answers.

"Massachusetts," says a girl whose family has lived in America since before the Revolutionary War.

"West Africa," says a boy whose grandparents were slaves.

"Sweden," "Ireland," "Germany," call out others.

Another little boy answers, "Japan." His great-grandparents were *Issei*, the first generation of Japanese to come to the United States. Like many Issei, this boy's great-grandfather probably came to the United States in the 1890s. Boarding a tramp steamer in Yokohama or another port, he began the long journey across the Pacific Ocean. About twenty days later he arrived in San Francisco.

Very likely, he was from a poor village in northern Japan. He had hoped to make a lot of money in America and go back to his village. Life was much harder in the United States than he had heard, though. He couldn't speak the language, and the only jobs he could get were hard labor—laying down railroad tracks, building factories, and cutting timber. He didn't mind the work because at home he had always worked long hours bent over in the flooded rice paddies. But at home there were family, friends, and a way of life he understood.

Still, he didn't give up. After a while he was able to get a small piece of farmland in the Sacramento Valley of California. Then he began to think about finding a wife. A family friend in Japan sent him the photograph of a young woman who lived in a village near his parents. He sent this woman his picture, and his parents did all they could to learn about her family. He knew that her parents were doing the same thing. Finally, both families agreed to a marriage, and the young woman sailed for America. She was now his wife, though the two of them had never spoken to each other.

He met her in San Francisco, and they drove to his home in the Sacramento Valley. Neither of them thought they had done anything unusual. Arranged marriages like theirs were the rule in Japan. He had been surprised when some Americans had told him that these marriages were a bad practice. They called his wife, and Japanese women like her, "Picture Brides." But he wondered, how else were you supposed to meet young women? How else could you find someone that your whole family could agree on? After all, marriage was a matter that concerned the whole family, not just the two people getting married.

The man and his wife worked hard on their farm, growing vegetables to sell in the cities. They were able to save a little of the money they earned. After a time, they had children.

An Issei's children were known as *Nisei*. That means they were the second generation of Japanese in the United States. The Nisei spoke Japanese to their parents, but they used English at school and in play.

Nisei had a foot in two worlds—Japan and America. Yet they lived in America, and its ways and dreams became their own. Some of them sent their children back to Japan to attend Japanese schools. Most, however, did not. Their ties with Japan were loosening.

The Japanese in the United States worried a great deal about the future—their own and their children's. Many Americans hated the Japanese. Some feared that Japanese farmers and fishermen would put them out of business. Others thought that the Japanese kept too much to themselves. They thought the Issei should open up more and not hang onto their old ways so strongly. Yet the Issei felt best having friends who celebrated the same holidays and spoke the same language.

Still other Americans, angry that their own lives had failed, blamed their troubles on the Japanese. They made fun of the way the Japanese looked and said America was only for white people. These same people hated American blacks and called them names. Indeed, to them anyone who wasn't white was to blame for their failures. Finding fault with others was easier than changing their own lives.

In 1906 the city of San Francisco passed a law that forced Japanese children to attend schools that separated them from other American students. Seven years later California passed a law that prevented the Japanese from buying land. Instead, they were forced to rent land or work for others. American fishermen tried to get a law passed stating that Japanese couldn't own fishing boats. Finally, in 1924, Congress passed a bill that would not allow Japanese to enter the United States because of their race. This law was called the Alien Exclusion Act.

The Issei wrote to their families about the racial prejudice in America. Japanese newspapers and magazines carried many articles about the problem. The Issei in America quietly tried to protect their families from the people who hated them. They said, *Shikata ga nai*, which meant, "Well, there's nothing that can be done." The Japanese in Japan, though, grew more and more angry about what they heard.

During the 1930s Japan became deeply involved in several wars. Japanese soldiers were fighting in China, Korea, Taiwan, and southeast Asia. Then on

December 7, 1941, Japanese planes bombed the U.S.
naval base Pearl Harbor in Hawaii.

Now Japan was at war with the United States.
Though they had feared trouble, the Japanese living
in America were as surprised as anyone about the
bombing. They had heard the rumors of war, and yet,
like other Americans, they had hoped for peace.

On February 19, 1942, President Roosevelt

changed the lives and futures of 110,000 Japanese living in the United States. On that date he signed Executive Order 9066. It forced the Japanese living in California, Oregon, Washington, and southern Arizona to go to places that were like prison camps. These camps were called War Relocation Authority Centers.

The Japanese sent to these camps had done

In Seattle, Washington, hundreds of onlookers watch Japanese-American families being marched to a train that will carry them to a relocation camp.

nothing wrong. Some officials, however, thought that they might be spies for Japan. And army leaders worried that these Japanese might help enemy soldiers if Japan attacked the West Coast of America.

The Federal Bureau of Investigation never uncovered a spy ring on the West Coast. Still, Japanese families were torn from their homes and sent to live in crowded barracks located in deserts or wetlands. There were camps in California, Arizona, Idaho, Wyoming, Colorado, Utah, and Arkansas. The Japanese lost most of their belongings, their homes, and their land, or had to sell them for a small part of what they were worth.

Japanese who were sent into the camps stayed there until 1946—four years behind barbed wire. They did the best they could, but life was hard. There was no privacy. Bathrooms were shared. Everyone ate together, and the food was often bad.

The Japanese in the camps did set up schools for their children. Japanese doctors and nurses took care of the sick, too. For many people, however, there was not enough to do. They tried to keep busy, but whatever they did seemed useless. It was a sad time they have never forgotten.

Because of their experiences in the camps, Japanese Americans later worked to change some American laws they thought were unfair. In 1950 the Emer-

(Top) Many of the special camps, such as this one at Manzanar, California, were located in a barren desert area. (Bottom) All of the camps were very crowded, as this scene from the barracks at the Granada Relocation Center in Amache, Colorado, shows.

gency Detention Act was passed by Congress. It said that prison camps could be set up if the president declared that they were needed. Anyone who was thought to be a threat to America's safety would be put in these camps. Lawyers for the Japanese-American Citizens League fought for many years to get rid of the act, and in 1971 Congress voted to do away with it. The Japanese Americans believed they had won a fight for the rights of all Americans.

Today about 600,000 Japanese Americans live in the United States. Two-thirds of them live in Hawaii and California. They have worked hard to rebuild their lives. Many of the *Sansei* and *Yonsei*, the third and fourth generations, have become important people in their communities. They are doctors, lawyers, business people, organizers, writers, and actors.

S.I. Hayakawa, a former college president, became a U.S. senator from California. Daniel Inouye has served as a U.S. senator from Hawaii, and Patsy Takemoto Mink has served that state as a U.S. representative. Isamu Noguchi, a sculptor, is of Japanese background. The architect of the World Trade Center in New York City, Minoru Yamasaki, is a Japanese American. And Tomi Kanazawa was the first Japanese American to play a leading role in the Metropolitan Opera Company.

Although there is still some prejudice against the

Japanese in the United States, many Japanese ways have become part of American life. Americans study the tea ceremony and *ikebana*, Japanese flower arranging. Some American businesses are trying the Japanese idea of encouraging all workers to feel that they have an important contribution to make to a company. Karate, judo, and aikido have become popular American sports. Many American cities have a Japanese garden in one of their parks. Nichiren Buddhism has become the religion of some Americans, as have forms of Zen Buddhism.

Americans once thought that the Japanese language was too difficult for them to learn. Today many colleges and universities and even some high schools are teaching classes in it.

People in the United States are also learning about Japanese ways from younger Japanese Americans. Older Japanese Americans belong to churches and clubs that are only for Japanese. They still feel most comfortable with their own people and say little about their lives. But the Sansei and Yonsei are telling other Americans about the Japanese-American experience through plays, novels, poems, and political organizations.

Today Japanese come to the United States from Japan to learn English, attend college, or work for a Japanese company. On Saturdays their children

Beautiful Japanese gardens and landscape arrangements can be found in many American city parks.

often go to Japanese schools where classes are taught in Japanese. Some of these visitors decide to stay and, in time, to become new American citizens.

America is a country of many peoples from many places around the world. Some of these peoples came freely in order to make money, to worship in their own way, or to find adventure. Others were forced to come as slaves. All of them brought valuable ways and ideas to their new land.

The people who came to America are like the roots of a tree. As the roots give the tree life, so the people have given the country life. The Japanese are one of these roots. In various ways they have helped America to grow and develop. By understanding the Japanese and their experience in the United States, Americans can better understand themselves.

Appendix A

Japanese Consulates in the United States and Canada

The Japanese Consulates in the United States and Canada want to help North Americans understand Japanese culture. They have brochures, maps, posters, and magazines for teachers. They have slides and films that can be borrowed free of charge. Their officers can speak to your group about Japan, or they can arrange for a qualified speaker in the area to attend your group. Contact the consulate nearest you for more information.

U.S. Consulates

Anchorage, Alaska
Consulate General of Japan
909 West Ninth Avenue, Suite 301
Anchorage, Alaska 99501
Phone (907) 279-8428

Atlanta, Georgia
Consulate General of Japan
400 Colony Square Building, Suite 1501
1201 Peachtree Street NE
Atlanta, Georgia 30361
Phone (404) 892-2700

Chicago, Illinois
Consulate General of Japan
Water Tower Place, Suite 950 E
845 North Michigan Avenue
Chicago, Illinois 60611
Phone (312) 280-0430

Los Angeles, California
Consulate General of Japan
250 East First Street, Suite 1507
Los Angeles, California 90012
Phone (213) 624-8305

New York, New York
Consulate General of Japan
280 Park Avenue
New York, New York 10017
Phone (212) 986-1600

Seattle, Washington
Consulate General of Japan
3110 Rainier Bank Tower
1301 Fifth Avenue
Seattle, Washington 98101
Phone (206) 682-9107

Washington, D.C.
Embassy of Japan
2520 Massachusetts Avenue NW
Washington, D.C. 20008
Phone (202) 234-2226

Canadian Consulates

Montreal, Quebec
    Consulate General of Japan
    1155 Dorchester Boulevard West, Suite 2701
    Montreal, Quebec H3B 2K9
    Phone (514) 866-3429

Toronto, Ontario
    Consulate General of Japan
    Toronto Dominion-Centre
    Post Office Box 10
    Toronto, Ontario M5K 1A1
    Phone (416) 363-7038

Vancouver, British Columbia
    Consulate General of Japan
    1177 Hastings Street West, Suite 1210
    Vancouver, British Columbia V6E 2K9
    Phone (604) 684-5868, 684-5869

Winnipeg, Manitoba
    Consulate General of Japan
    Fifth Floor, Three Lakeview Square
    185 Carlton Street
    Winnipeg, Manitoba R3C 3J1
    Phone (204) 943-5554

Appendix B

Make Your Own Kimono!

An American company makes and sells patterns for the *yukata*, a Japanese summer kimono, and for Japanese farmer's clothing. The patterns include information on how the outfits are worn as well as background on traditional dyeing and decoration techniques.

Write to Folkwear Patterns, Box 3798, San Rafael, California 94902, for more information.

Appendix C

Japanese Hiragana Symbols

ん	わ	ら	や	ま	は	な	た	さ	か	あ
	り			み	ひ	に	ち	し	き	い
	る	ゆ		む	ふ	ぬ	つ	す	く	う
	れ			め	へ	ね	て	せ	け	え
を	ろ	よ		も	ほ	の	と	そ	こ	お

n	wa	ra	ya	ma	ha	na	ta	sa	ka	a
		ri		mi	hi	ni	chi	shi	ki	i
		ru	yu	mu	hu	nu	tsu	su	ku	u
		re		me	he	ne	te	se	ke	e
	wo	ro	yo	mo	ho	no	to	so	ko	o

To match the symbols with their English forms, start at the top right side of the page. Read down the first column. Then begin at the top of the next column, continuing on to the left.

Glossary

aikido—a Japanese fighting sport; players use holds and throws to win a match

Ainu—probably the earliest settlers in Japan

Akemashite omedetoo gozaimasu—"Happy New Year"

Bon odori—a circle dance performed by people of all ages at the Obon festival

booru—the Japanese baseball term for ball

Bunraku—Japanese puppet plays featuring large costumed puppets handled by people who can be seen by the audience, and a chanter who speaks all the lines in the play

bushido—"The Way of the Warrior"; this code called for samurai warriors to be brave, true to friends, and fearless of death

chanko—a meat, chicken, or fish, and vegetable dish eaten by sumo wrestlers to help them gain weight

chichi—an informal name for father

daimyo—kings who once ruled in various parts of Japan

dango—rice dumplings that are eaten on the last night of the Obon festival

dashi—Japanese soup stock

fouru—the Japanese baseball term for foul

Fuji-san—the Japanese name for Mount Fuji, Japan's highest mountain

futon—the quiltlike bedding in which most Japanese sleep

genkan—the entrance way to a Japanese house

geta—wooden sandals

gohan—rice

hakama—old-fashioned divided skirts worn by kendo players

hanami—the flower-viewing trips that the Japanese take in the spring

haniwa—red, baked clay statues that were placed around the tombs of ancient Japanese chieftains

hiragana—a smooth and flowing form of Japanese writing that is like handwriting

hisimochi—rice cakes that are placed on special display shelves on Girl's Day (March 3)

hitto—the Japanese baseball term for hit

Hyakuinshu—a famous collection of one hundred Japanese poems

ikebana—flower arranging

Issei—the first generation of Japanese in the United States

Itte irasshai—"See you later!"

Itte kimasu—"Yes. See you in a while."

judo—a traditional Japanese fighting sport; players use holds and throws to win a match

junihitoe—a dress worn by wealthy women during the Heian period (A.D. 794–1185); the dress was made of twelve kimonos carefully layered over one another

kabuki—traditional Japanese plays performed by human actors in a highly formal manner

kagami mochi—a special cake made of pounded rice that is eaten at the New Year's festival

kaishi—special paper napkins used in the tea ceremony

kami—the general name used for the gods of the Shinto religion

kappa—spirits who are said to live in ponds, lakes, and streams

karate—a Japanese form of self-defense in which kicks and punches are used to disable an attacker

katakana—a hard and square form of Japanese writing that is like printing

kendo—Japanese fencing

kimono—a traditional Japanese robe made of cotton or silk that has long, square sleeves and is tied with a sash

kitsune—the fox who is the subject of many Japanese stories and sayings

kitsunebi—"fox light"; the Japanese name for will-o-the-wisp, a strange darting light sometimes seen in forests

kitsune ga bakasaseta—"to be tricked by a fox"; a Japanese expression meaning "I've been fooled."

kitsune udon—"fox noodles"; a Japanese dish made of large white noodles topped with fried soybean cake

koinobori—huge carplike paper fish that are flown on Children's Day (May 5)

Koohaku Utagasen—"song battle of Red against White"; a TV program broadcast on New Year's Eve in which two teams of Japanese singing stars compete against each other

kotatsu—a low table with an electric heating bulb beneath its top; people seated on the floor can place their legs and feet under the table to keep warm

kyoiku mama—"education mama"; a Japanese mother who pushes her children very, very hard to do well in school

matsutake—a large Japanese mushroom that grows only in pine forests

Meiji—"Enlightened Rule"; the name given to the period from 1868 to 1912 when Emperor Mutsuhito ruled Japan; after 1867 Mutsuhito himself was called Emperor Meiji

miso—a fermented soybean product that is used in Japanese soups

Mount Hiei—a Buddhist temple on the outskirts of Kyoto that was famous for its fighting priests

Nambanjin—"Southern Barbarians"; the name the Japanese gave to the Europeans who came to Japan in 1543

Nan mai o kitte iru?—"How many layers [of clothing] are you wearing?"

Nisei—the second generation of Japanese in the United States

Noh—traditional Japanese dance-plays dealing with heroic actions, and featuring masked actors, a chorus, and beautiful costumes

obi—a wide sash used to tie a kimono

Obon—a Buddhist festival for the spirits of the dead that is usually held in the middle of July or August

o-chazuke—a Japanese dish in which green tea is poured over cooked rice

ojiisan—an old farmer

Okaeri—"Welcome home."

okonomiyaki—vegetable pancakes

o-miyage—a souvenir

on—the feeling of love and responsibility that Japanese children have for their parents

oni—Japanese devils who are said to have three fingers and toes, and, sometimes, three eyes and horns

origami—the art of paper folding

O-shogatsu—the name for the New Year's festival that is held on January 1

otosan—a formal word for father; it is a term of respect and praise

o-tosu—the sweet spiced wine drunk by the Japanese at their first meal of the New Year

oyako domburi—a bowl of rice covered with a chicken and egg mixture

o-zoni—the soup that is eaten by the Japanese at their first meal of the New Year

pachinko—a Japanese game played on pinball machines

puure booru—the Japanese baseball expression for "Play Ball"

sake—rice wine

samurai—one of a number of warriors who served Japanese kings during the twelfth and thirteenth centuries

Sansei—the third generation of Japanese in the United States

Shichi-go-san—a Japanese festival held on November 15 for three-year-old boys and girls, five-year-old girls, and seven-year-old boys

Shikata ga nai—"Well, there's nothing that can be done."

Shinkansen—the "Bullet Train" that travels 130 miles per hour

shogun—the name given to the military men who ruled Japan from 1192 to 1867

Showa—the name given to the period of time Emperor Hirohito has ruled Japan; Hirohito became emperor in 1926 and 1982 is year fifty-seven of his Showa

soba—buckwheat noodles eaten at the last meal of the year

soroban—a simple, wooden, hand-operated computer

sturiki—the Japanese baseball term for strike

sumo—a traditional Japanese wrestling sport

tabi—ankle high white socks divided at the big toe of each foot

Tadaima—"Hey! I'm home."

Tanabata—a children's festival held on July 7

tatami—the straw mats that are used to cover the floors of Japanese houses

tempura—vegetables or seafood coated with batter and fried in oil

tengu—magical creatures with long noses who are said to live in the mountains of Japan

tofu—soybean curds

tokonoma—a small wall opening in a Japanese house in which a beautiful painting or a flower arrangement is placed

tsukimi—the word for moon watching, something the Japanese like to do during the fall

tsuru—paper cranes made to honor the lives and spirits of the children of Hiroshima and Nagasaki who were killed by the atomic bomb during World War II

tsuyu—the rainy season in Japan that begins in June and lasts until early July

typhoon—a hurricanelike storm that brings strong winds and heavy rains to Japan during the fall

utakaruta—a very old card game; players try to match cards that are printed with the lines from famous Japanese poems

yamauba—female goblins who are said to live in the mountains of Japan

Yayoi—the second group of people to settle in Japan; arriving sometime between the second and third centuries B.C., they brought wet-rice farming, the potter's wheel, and bronze and iron tools from Asia to Japan

Yonsei—the fourth generation of Japanese in the United States

yu—the hiragana symbol for hot water that is displayed on a curtain hanging outside a public bath

yukata—a summer kimono

Selected Bibliography

Berger, Donald Paul, ed. *Folk Songs of Japanese Children*. Tokyo: Charles E. Tuttle Co., 1969.

Cox, Miriam. *The Three Treasures, Myths of Old Japan*. New York: Harper and Row, 1964.

Davis, Daniel S. *Behind Barbed Wire: The Imprisonment of Japanese Americans During World War II*. New York: E.P. Dutton, 1981. (Grades 4-7)

Dunn, Charles J. *Everyday Life in Traditional Japan*. Tokyo: Charles E. Tuttle Co., 1969.

Epstein, Sam, and Epstein, Beryl. *A Year of Japanese Festivals*. Champaign, Ill.: Garrard Publishing Co., 1974.

Kasahara, Kunihiko. *Creative Origami*. Tokyo: Japan Publications, 1977.

Kuhaulua, Jesse, with Wheeler, John. *Takamiyama, The World of Sumo*. Tokyo: Kodansha International, 1973.

Obojski, Robert. *The Rise of Japanese Baseball Power*. Radnor, Pa.: Chilton Book Co., 1975.

Piegott, Julia. *Japanese Mythology*. London: Hamlyn Publishing Group, 1969.

Tsuji, Shizuo, with Sutherland, Mary. *Japanese Cooking: A Simple Art*. Tokyo: Kodansha International, 1980.

Index

ABOUT THE AUTHOR

Photo by Wes Hohlbein

"America is a country of many cultures," writes Judith Davidson. "We need to understand our own roots as well as the roots of friends and neighbors in our communities."

Ms. Davidson is well qualified to write about the heritage of Japanese Americans, having lived, taught, and studied in Japan. From 1974 to 1976 she taught English in Kyoto and also studied at Kyoto Japanese Language School and Tezukayama Women's College. After returning from Japan, she worked for the Consulate General of Japan in Portland, Oregon, preparing materials for schools and libraries on Japanese customs and history. She has also taken coursework in Japanese children's literature at the University of Oregon and received a B.A. in Japanese Studies from Antioch University.

Currently a writer who lives in New York, Ms. Davidson has translated two Japanese children's stories into English. Her articles have appeared in newspapers and magazines. She is presently working on a novel for older children.